Playing
CHESS

Playing
CHESS

BOB WADE

Collier Books
Macmillan Publishing Company
New York

Macmillan Publishing Company
866 Third Avenue, New York, N.Y. 10022

Library of Congress Cataloging in Publication Data
Wade, Robert Graham.
Playing chess.
Bibliography: p.
Includes indexes.
1. Chess. I. Title.
GV1445.W17   1984   794.1'2   84-15543
ISBN 0–02–011980–1 (pbk.)

Macmillan books are available at special discounts for bulk purchases for sales promotions, premiums, fund-raising, or educational use. For details, contact:

> Special Sales Director
> Macmillan Publishing Company
> 866 Third Avenue
> New York, N.Y. 10022

10 9 8 7 6 5 4 3 2

Printed in the United Kingdom

Contents

Preface

International Master Bob Wade O.B.E. is one of the world's most experienced chess teachers. He has been the chief coach for promising young players of the British Chess Federation for many years and he is also chief arbiter of the Commonwealth Chess Association.

Bob has packed into this book his most important thoughts about the teaching, history and psychology of chess. In addition he has briefly elucidated the moves of the game and explained basic strategies, tactics and key opening variations.

Whether the reader is a complete beginner or already an expert, he will find much of value and interest here from Bob Wade's accumulated store of chess wisdom.

Ray Keene,
London, May 1 1984

1 The moves and their history

Chess, as we know it, is about five hundred years old. The present moves of the chessmen have remained about the same since the mid-1500s.

But chess itself is much older. We don't know exactly when civilisations began to substitute war games and board games and armchair strategists for war itself. There is evidence that the 8 by 8 board was in use even before the Romans came to Britain, though for what games it is not certain. The chessboard of 64 squares and its two chess armies was in use in the Sanskrit areas of Indo–Pakistan about AD 550. Its aim then, as it is today, was to capture the opposing king. It is this singular objective that distinguishes chess from other games.

In Sanskrit chess the pieces may have represented the four arms of war—the chariot, the elephant, the horseman and the foot-soldier—plus a king and minister. Today the corresponding names are rook, bishop, knight and pawn, together with king and queen.

We know something about the four-handed game of Chaturanga—played around AD 600—in which dice were thrown. That a dice has six sides and chess six differing pieces may be no coincidence. If you threw one you moved the pawn. Two meant the horseman could move. Three—the elephant, and so on. . . .

Chess came to Europe in three ways. From Northern India it was passed on to Persia—it has been suggested as a gift between kings. Possibly it was taken back to the Caliphates of Baghdad by Arab traders journeying to Persia, or by the Arab conquerors of Persia (AD 640–650). The Arabs, as they expanded west under the impetus of the Islamic faith, took it along North Africa and the Moors introduced the game into Spain. Independently the crusaders brought it back to Western Europe as they returned from the Holy Land. And the Mediterranean traders carried it via Asia Minor through the Balkans and the Greek Islands to Italy. It was in cities of Italy that chess underwent revolutionary changes in the late 1400s and first half of the 1500s. Only the rook and the knight moves of early chess survived intact. All the other pieces increased their scope.

Another European influence on the game is the change made

from the pieces being the symbolic representations of the elements of an army to the trappings of a royal court. The elephant of India became a bishop to the British, *un fou*, or court jester to the French, *ein laufer* meaning a runner or messenger to the Germans, and so on. . . . The term queen (or lady in other languages) is a European conception. It must show the greater outward importance of the woman in European councils! In older times and other lands this piece was the minister and had a more limited motion than the king.

There are two chess armies: one has dark-coloured chess men and the other light-shaded. We refer to the two sides as Black and White, but it's hard on the eyes to play for any length of time with such absolute contrasts. The same objection must apply to the squares on the board.

The Board
It is probably a surprise to most chessplayers to learn that the original boards were not chequered. The earliest may have been merely lines drawn on the ground; later the squares were divided by lines sewn on to cloth. The chequered board was not so necessary. Our rook (their chariot or boat) was the only far-ranging piece.

Then, no other piece went further than two squares diagonally. The modern bishop and eye have to travel along complete diagonals, and that makes the alternate colouring of squares essential.

We moderns have added one rule to the laying out of the board: it must be placed between the players in such a way that the corner square nearest their right hands is a white one (diag 1).

The Rooks
The rooks—their appearance makes you think of a castle—start on the corner squares (diag 2).

The rooks are the wingers of the chessboard; in old Sanskrit armies they were the chariots, mostly stationed on and racing down the flanks. In some countries where chariots were unknown, the piece was symbolised by other objects, such as a boat to the people of Bengal and the Slav tribes of the Volga/Don rivers, or a castle to the Italians of the Middle Ages. Scholars are divided on the origin of our word 'Rook'. One thought it was Old Persian for a chariot.

The Knights
Next to the rooks go the horsemen, the cavalry, the knights as we call them (diag 3).

The Bishops
The bishops, these are the ones with the split in the head. They go next to the knights (diag 4).

They were the elephants in the old-time armies, but to the fifteenth-century Europeans the elephants were almost mythical creatures. From the sketch of the arabic piece you can trace the elephant's tusks. Does the split emanate from this?

The King and Queen
The two remaining squares on each back rank are for the king and queen.

The queen always starts on a square of her own colour. The white queen is placed on a white square and the black queen on a dark one (diag 5).

The kings take the remaining squares (diag 6).

Checkmate
Though not as powerful a piece as the queen, the king is the most important. If he is attacked and cannot escape capture he is said to be checkmated. Then the game is, at once, lost.

The Pawns
Each side's eight pawns are stationed on the row of squares in front of their pieces. Our word 'pawn' is a corrupted form of the French word *pion* meaning foot-soldier (diag 7).

Starting Position Summary
Re-checking where the pieces start—board's nearest right hand corner
is a white square, rooks are put in the corners, knights next to them,
then the bishops, queen is put on her own colour and the king has
the remaining square; the pawns are lined up in front.

Naming the Squares
Each square is described by its co-ordinates, built up from the letters
a to h and the numbers 1 to 8, which diagram 8 illustrates. For
instance the corner squares on which the white rooks always begin,
are a1 and h1, while the black rooks start from a8 and h8. The white
army starts from the first and second ranks, and the black one on the
seventh and eighth. In diagram 8 random squares are indicated.

8

The Moves—General
All the back rank pieces move forward or backwards; the pawns can
only move forward.

Only a knight can jump over another chessman to a square beyond.

You are not to move to a square already occupied by one of your
own men.

You capture by taking the opponent's piece off the board and
moving your own man into its place.

Rook's Move
Rooks move to or take on any square along its file or rank. A **file**
is a row of squares stretching between your opponent's and your
own starting position; a **rank** is a row of squares from the left hand
to the right hand side of the board. (In other words, ranks and files
are at right angles to each other.)

A rook placed at a4 on an empty board can move along the file to a5, a6, a7, a8 or to a3, a2 and a1, or along the rank to b4, c4, d4, e4, f4, g4 and h4.

In diagram 9, the white rook at a4 can take the black rook at a7, but cannot go to a8; and it cannot move to f4 (occupied by the white pawn) nor beyond it to g4 and h4.

Exercising the Rook As an exercise, take black pawns and place one on each of the following squares: b3, b6, c5, e3, f7, f6, h5, h7 and put a white rook on c2 (diag 10); with the black pawns not moving White is able to make eight consecutive moves with the rook, capturing a black pawn each move.

To do the exercise, cast your eyes along each square of the rank and file on which the rook stands. You are correct if you take the pawns at c5, h5, h7, f7, f6, b6, b3 and e3 in that order. Repeat this exercise until the action of looking along the ranks and files and making the captures comes quickly.

In the exercise in diagram 11 you are asked to name the square to which you would move the rook in order to attack the white king. Answer—to d8 square. This puts the white king in check. Check is a corruption of the Persian word *shah*, meaning king. It used to be good manners to warn the opponent when his king was attacked; but nowadays at international and club levels this courtesy is dispensed with. The less said, the better—that is the contemporary attitude.

Bishop's Move

Bishops move to or take on any square along one of the diagonals upon which they are standing. Diagonals are the straight rows of squares of the same colour with corners touching.

A black bishop, placed on f6 on an open board, as in diagram 12, can move to e7, d8, g7, h8, g5, h4, e5, d4, c3, b2 and a1 or take a white piece on one of these squares.

12

Exercising the Bishop (diag 13): put a black bishop on g7 and indicate which squares it would need to be moved to, in order to check (i.e. be on the same diagonal as) the white king on the following squares, 1) e1, 2) b8, 3) b6, 4) h4, 5) c1. Answers: 1) Bishop to c3, 2) ♗ to e5, 3) ♗d4, 4) ♗f6 and 5) either ♗b2 or ♗h6.

Queen's Move

The queen is the most powerful piece on the modern chessboard. It moves and makes captures exactly as the rooks or bishops do.

Exercising the Queen Put a black queen on d8, white knight on h2 and white pawn on b5 (diag 14). Find a square to play the queen to, which attacks both knight and pawn.

Answer: the queen can move to h8 and h4 to attack the knight down the file, to d2 to attack it along the rank, and to d6, c7 and b8 to attack it along the diagonal. The queen can attack the pawn from d5, g5, a5, b6, b8, e8, d7 and d3. The only coinciding square and correct answer is queen to b8 (♛d8–b8). With White having a pawn at b2 and a knight at g4 (diag 15), make one move with a black queen from f7 to attack both. Answer: Black queen goes to g7 (♛f7–g7).

King's Move

The king is the side's most important piece despite its very limited mobility. It can move or take one square away either forward, backwards, sideways or diagonally. A king on e1 (diag 16) may be moved to d1, d2, e2, f2 and f1. A king on e5 (diag 17) could be moved to d4, d5, d6, e6, f6, f5, f4 and e4.

The King is Dead—Checkmate

To win the opponent's king is the objective of the game of chess. Indeed, if the king is checked, and there is no way its capture can be delayed or averted, it is said to be checkmated and game is immediately over.

The king must not remain in check on the move succeeding the one by which it was attacked.

Also the king must not be played on to a square where it could be captured.

The word checkmate is a centuries-slurred expression from the Persian language for *Shah manad*—the king is ambushed, and the Arabic word *mat*—dead. In fact the conception of checkmate seems to date back to Persian times. Before then the game ended with the physical capture of the king. The black king is in check to the white rook in diagram 18. One can consider three different ways of countering check. They are:

1) Take the checking piece. Here, the black bishop at c3 can take the white rook.

2) Interpose a third piece. The black bishop, when it is played to a5 shuts off the check.

3) Move the king out of check. The king can be played to b7, b6 or take the white knight at b5.

In diagram 19 the white king is checkmated. It is checked by the rook at a8. This cannot be captured. There's no interposition. The king cannot move to squares b1 or b2 as they are commanded by the other black rook. The game is over.

Find a move that checkmates the black king in each of diagrams 20, 21, 22 and 23. Answers: 20)—rook to h6; 21)—rook to h5 (the black king cannot move to the squares g8, g7 or g6 covered by the white king); 22)—bishop to f6; 23)—rook to h8, where it is protected by the bishop.

Illegal Moves

If, after moving, you have left or put your king in check, or have made some other illegal move, the game is returned to the position before the illegality happened and a legal move is substituted; if possible, the move correcting the illegality will be made with the piece(s) first touched/taken at the time.

Knight's Move

The knight's move looks more complicated than it really is (diag 24). It has an L-shaped leap. It goes two squares along any file or rank, and then, as part of the same move, continues one square to the left or right. Diagrams 25, 26 and 27 give examples of its move.

Like a good horseman, the knight is able to jump over obstacles. For instance in diagram 28, it jumps over g3, on to g2, turns and completes the move by taking the white rook at h2. An even more

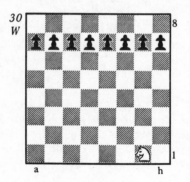

deadly example of its jumping ability is given in diagram 29; White can give mate by playing his knight to f7; all the black king's flight squares are occupied by Black's own pieces. We describe this type of finish as a smothered mate.

Practice for the Knight
The black pawns stay fixed on their squares throughout the next test (diag 30); the white knight is on its original square. White has 18 consecutive moves in which to capture all eight of Black's pawns.

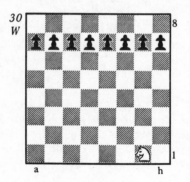

Sample answer: The knight is played to f3, to g5, takes h7, back to g5, takes f7, to e5, takes d7, to c5, takes b7, to d6, to b5, takes a7, to b5, takes c7, to d5, takes e7, to f5 and finally, takes g7. Practise this until the knight's move comes smoothly.

Moves Summarised
Ranks and files for the rooks, diagonals for the bishops, the queen

moves like a rook or bishop, L-shaped leaps for the knight and one careful square for the king.

Pawn Moves

Each side starts with eight pawns lined up in front of the pieces. Mostly a pawn moves one square straight forward (diag 31). It cannot retreat. Each pawn can be moved either one or two squares (diag 32) ahead on its first move; the privilege of moving the pawn two squares dates back to the 1300s and 1400s—part of the Italians' impatience with the number of moves it took for the two chess armies to get to grips in olden chess.

Pawns do *not* take in the same direction as they move. Remember they represent the foot-soldiers of ancient armies; these soldiers would be guarded from frontal attack by their shields; when they met face to face, there would not be any obvious point of penetration. On the chessboard in such circumstances they stay put; in diagram 33 the white and black pawns cannot be moved. Their attacking stroke is the oblique jab forward round the side of the shield and this is symbolised in chess.

A pawn captures one square diagonally forward. In diagram 34 the pawn can take the knight; in diagram 35 the pawn can take the bishop but not the queen.

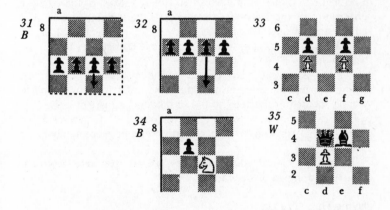

As a pawn cannot move back, what happens to it when it reaches the far row? There's promotion for it. It can be exchanged as part of its arrival move, for either a queen (usual), or a rook, bishop or knight. It does not matter if you have a queen on the board already; you can have a second; indeed you could have as many as nine queens on your side; in practice two should suffice. If you cannot find a second black queen in your set, use an upturned rook or two pawns on the same square or a lump of sugar or something that distinguishes the unit.

Pawn Move Recapped
A pawn moves forward one or two squares on its first move and one square thereafter; it captures one square diagonally forward; and at the far end it is promoted.

White Starts
In modern chess, the player with the white pieces always begins the game. For many reasons it is more convenient that one colour should always begin, e.g. easier recording and classification of important games.

Writing the Moves
The algebraic system using the letters a–h and figures 1–8 for naming the squares on the chessboard is the most widely used in the world. The descriptive notation, in which the squares are named according to the starting squares of pieces, is still common in English- and Spanish-speaking countries. This notation is described on p. 156. Both systems date back to about the eleventh century. But there is a steady switch from the descriptive to the algebraic systems in both the British Isles and Northern America. Most of the younger generation use the algebraic. From a publisher's point of view it is simpler and cheaper (perhaps as much as 25 per cent cheaper) to print. With paper costs soaring the inevitable change may have to be speeded up.

A move is a piece being played from one square to another. In writing the move in long fashion the same order is followed—piece symbol, square of departure, to (–) or takes (x), square of arrival.

Piece symbols are ♚ for king, ♛ for queen, ♜ for rook, ♝ for bishop and ♞ for knight; if there is no prefixing piece symbol, it's a pawn move.

The square co-ordinates (examples: a1, e4, g6) were described on p. 13 and shown on diagram 8.

Playing Through a Game
If White's first move in a game is pawn in front of king two squares, that pawn starts its move on e2 and finishes on e4; in long fashion that is written 1 e2–e4. If Black replies with knight on g8 to f6 (attacking White's advanced pawn) that's written 1 . . . ♞g8–f6. When White defends by knight on b1 to c3 the score sheet would show 2 ♞b1–c3. Black's next move, pawn on d7 to d5–2 . . . d7–d5. White's third move is pawn on e4 takes on d5–3 e4xd5; Black's knight recaptures—3 . . . ♞f6xd5; White plays bishop out

THE RED KNIGHTS

EVENT... Baden-Baden, International Tournament DATE 25.4.1925

WHITE... Réti ... BLACK... Alekhine

WHITE	BLACK		WHITE	BLACK
1. g2-g3	e7-e5	27.	Nd4-f3	c6xb5
2. Ng1-f3	e5-e4	28.	Qc4xb5	Nd5-c3
3. Nf3-d4	d7-d5	29.	Qb5xb7	Qc7xb7
4. d2-d3	e4xd3	30.	Nc5xb7	Nc3xe2+
5. Qd1xd3	Ng8-f6	31.	Kg1-h2	Nf6-e4
6. Bf1-g2	Bf8-b4+	32.	Rc1-c4	Ne4xf2
7. Bc1-d2	Bb4xd2+	33.	Bh1-g2	Bg4-e6
8. Nb1xd2	O-O	34.	Rc4-c2	Nf2-g4+
9. c2-c4	Nb8-a6	35.	Kh2-h3	Ng4-e5+
10. c4xd5	Na6-b4	36.	Kh3-h2	Re3xf3
11. Qd3-c4	Nb4xd5	37.	Rd2xe2	Ne5-g4+
12. Nd2-b3	c7-c6	38.	Kh2-h3	Ng4-e3+
13. O-O	Rf8-e8	39.	Kh3-h2	Ne3xc2
14. Rf1-d1	Bc8-g4	40.	Bg2xf3	Nc2-d4
15. Rd1-d2	Qd8-c8	41.	Resigned	
16. Nb3-c5	Bg4-h3	42.		
17. Bg2-f3	Bh3-g4	43.		
18. Bf3-g2	Bg4-h3	44.		
19. Bg2-f3	Bh3-g4	45.		
20. Bf3-h1	h7-h5	46.		
21. b2-b4	a7-a6	47.		
22. Ra1-c1	h5-h4	48.		
23. a2-a4	h4xg3	49.		
24. h2xg3	Qc8-c7	50.		
25. b4-b5	a6xb5	51.		
26. a4xb5	Re8-e3	52.		

attacking the knight again—4 ♗f1–c4; Black's knight takes knight—
4 . . . ♘d5xc3; White does not take back, but brings his queen
out—5 ♕d1–f3; Black tries to save his knight 5 . . . ♘c3–a4; White's
queen takes a pawn near Black's king with check—6 ♕f3xf7+ (+ for
check); Black's king moves—6 . . . ♔e8–d7; White's queen checks at

f5–7 ♕f7–f5+; the black king is played to c6–7 . . . ♚d7–c6;
White's queen checks at b5–8 ♕f5–b5+; Black's king has one
move–8 . . . ♚c6–d6; White's queen gives checkmate–9 ♕b5–d5
mate (diag 36).

In the shorter form of the algebraic notation the game would be
written 1 e4 ♘f6 2 ♘c3 d5 3 ed ♘xd5 4 ♗c4 ♘xc3 5 ♕f3 ♘a4?
(? by commentator for a weak move) 6 ♕xf7+ ♚d7 7 ♕f5+ ♚c6
8 ♕b5+ ♚d6 9 ♕d5 mate. Only the arrival square is mentioned.
Some reference to the departure square would be made, if two
different pieces could end up on the arrival square, e.g. from diagram
37, ♖a5xa8 is shortened to ♖axa8 or ♖5xa8, and ♘b6xa8 is written
♘6xa8 or ♘bxa8. Note that White's 3rd move was written in short
form as ed; this is decoded as White's pawn on the e-file takes something black on the d-file.

The Four Moves Checkmate Game
(The pieces are set up ready to start a game; the corner square
nearest your right hand is white).

A conventional beginning. White plays **1 e2–e4**; it opens the door
for the bishop and the queen to emerge. Black replies similarly:
1 . . . e7–e5.

White's second move brings the bishop into play: **2 ♗f1–c4**, and
Black copies with **2 . . . ♗f8–c5**.

Next White plays the queen out along the diagonal as far as it can
go; **3 ♕d1–h5**. It's bearing on three of Black's pawns, one in the
centre unprotected, one next to the king only partially protected
and the one in front of the black rook which is adequately guarded.
Black replies **3 . . . d7–d6** (diag 38). He's seen the threat to his
central pawn; he's missed the more important one.

White plays **4 ♕h7xf7** and announces checkmate. The queen is
attacking the black king and cannot be taken by it—the king cannot
move on to the diagonal of White's bishop at c4. White's queen

covers also Black's three flight squares (f8, e7 and d7). It really is checkmate.

Chess games are lost through mistakes being made. What was Black's mistake? After 1 e4 e5 1 ♗c4 ♗c5 3 ♕h5 Black can defend both the attacked points (e5 and f7) in his position by 3 . . . ♕e7.

The Two Move Game

The next game shows the shortest possible road to checkmate. White starts 1 g2–g4; that's not nearly as good as moving one of the central pawns (c, d, e or f); moving the g-pawn one square is safer. In my knowledge no first class game has ever opened with the edge pawns being played to a4, h4 or h3.

The game continues 1 . . . e7–e5! (! means a good move) 2 f3?? (?? = very bad move). This opens up a line of approach to White's king—along the diagonal e1–f2–g3–h4 (diag 39). Black can checkmate by 2 . . . ♕d8–h4. The white king cannot be moved off the diagonal and there's no piece placed so as to be interposed between it and the black queen nor to capture the queen. This particular game is bluntly named Fool's Mate.

Special Moves—Castling

(In giving rook and king moves earlier in this chapter I deliberately omitted the special move involving both these pieces in order that L-readers could get started on a game.)

Castling is carried out from diagram 40 by placing the king two squares along the back rank (♔e1–g1), and then placing the rook involved (in this case h1) over the king and on to the square next beyond (f1), both operations together counting as a single move. (Diag 41). N.B. The king should be moved first.

The castling move can be made either way along the rank—and in doing it the king is always played two squares, e.g. it's ♔e8—c8 together with ♖a8—d8 (diag 42).

In the form that I have described it, the castling move dates from the fifteenth/sixteenth centuries; it seems to be derived from a much older king's leap in which the king was allowed, once during a game, to make a knight's move.

There are five conditions attached to the modern castling move. You cannot castle:

1 if the king has already moved during the game;
2 if the rook, being used, has already moved;
3 while the king is in check, as in diagram 43 to the bishop;
4 if the king has to cross over a square on which it could be taken. (Diagram 44 shows the white rook at f5 attacking the square f8—Black cannot castle yet)
5 while there is a piece on a square between the king and rook, as in diagram 45.

Re-capping: You can't castle if the king has moved, or with a rook that's moved, or while in check, or if the king jumps over a contested square, or if there is something between. Method is king two squares and rook over it to next door.

The special castling moves are written as **0—0** for castling on the short side (♔e1—g1/♔e8—g8) and **0—0—0** for castling on the long side (♔e1—c1/♔e8—c8).

Special Moves—Pawns taking En Passant
Pawn taking en passant or pawn taking in passing is the least known and most misunderstood operation in the laws of chess.

The initial double move for each pawn dates back to the 1400s, though it didn't become standardised until about the mid 1500s. During this time, it was found, there was a tendency for the two step move to lead to blocked pawn chains—something akin to the trench warfare of 1914-18. That didn't suit the dashing Italians, who invented the pawn taking pawn en passant capture. This ensured that when a pawn was moved two squares on its initial move it would not evade capture by an opponent's pawn on an adjacent file.

In diagram 46, if White pushes his pawn to b3 the black pawn at c4 can take it. If White plays the pawn at once two squares, the black pawn at c4 can still take it. The procedure is as follows: on the move succeeding 1 b2—b4 only, Black pushes the white pawn b4 back to b3 and, as part of the same move, captures it by 1 . . . c4xb3.

In diagram 47 Black plays 1 . . . h7—h5 and, on the very next move, White pushes the black pawn back to h6 and plays g5xh6; Black can continue 2 . . . g7xh6 and the game goes on.

Some Perspective
Now that a knowledge of the moves has been acquired one can set about building up experience by playing games. Before one can expect to beat Anatoly Karpov for his world title there lies toil, success, disappointments and study. One can start augmenting one's experience by a study of the techniques and ideas of the masters—most of their important achievements in the recorded moves of their games.

Chess is not so much an intellectual pastime as, at its best, a tough unrelenting tussle which will draw upon the full physical, mental and nervous qualities of the individuals involved.

Basic Attacking Methods
As a further step on the chess ladder one can gain a knowledge of basic methods of attacking. The three games that have been included so far in this chapter have shown straightforward attacks directed against a single target—the king. Another effective form of attack occurs when a move can be directed against two targets— a double attack. It can arise in a variety of shapes.

There is the knight fork. The knight is checking the black king in diagram 48 and, at the same time, it is also attacking the rook.

The bishop on b5 is pinning the rook on d7 against the black king in diagram 49. It is illegal for the rook to move, as that would expose the black king to capture. It would also be a pin if the black king was replaced by a queen; Black could not afford to move the rook as the queen is much more valuable than the bishop.

To the housewife, a skewer was a wooden and later a metal rod pushed through old-fashioned roasts of beef to hold them in shape. To a chess-player, a skewer is the action of the black rook in diagram 50 through the white king—which as the most important piece has to give way—leaving the knight in the rook's path.

I want to draw your attention to the position, in diagram 51, of the white king at d2 in relation to the black rook at d8. Move the black knight at d5 anywhere and the white king is in check, a check which must be attended to—in the meantime what damage will the knight be inflicting? All such uncovering manoeuvres are termed discovered attacks, and, in this particular instance, a discovered check. What knight move would Black play? We would examine all eight squares to which the knight could be played—e3, f4, f6, e7, c7, c3, b4, b6; best seems 1 . . . ♘d5–b6+ 2 ♔ moves ♘b6xa4 winning the bishop.

In all these preliminary examples of double attack, the king has

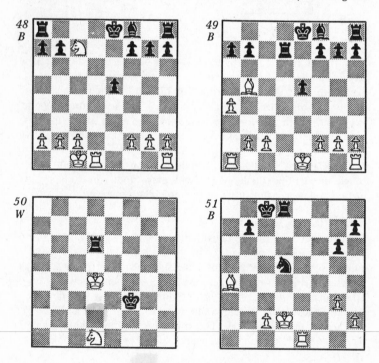

been included as one of the targets. This is merely for emphasis; forks, pins, skewers and discovered attacks can involve any piece.

Value of pieces
Which piece is the most valuable to win?

Practically all one's pieces can be sacrificed if this leads to the opposing king being checkmated—diagram 52 illustrates an exotic example. White forces mate by 1 ♕e3–h6+ ♔g7xh6 2 h5xg6+ ♔h6–g5 3 ♖h1–h5+ ♔g5xh5 4 f3–f4+ ♘d4xe2 5 ♘d5–f6+ ♔h5–h6 6 ♖b1–h1+ ♔h6–g7 7 ♘f6–e8+ ♖f8xe8 8 ♖h1xh7+ and 9 ♖h7xf7 mate. White sacrificed queen, rook, bishop and knight. There are other tries for Black, e.g. 1 ... ♔h8 2 ♕xh7+, 3 h5xg6++ (double check), 4 ♖xh7 mate; or 2 ... ♔g7 3 ♖xh7 mate; or 4 ... ♔ moves 5 ♖h1+ and two more rook moves at most; 5 ... ♔h4 6 ♖h1+ ♔h3 6 ♖xh3 mate. Therefore it is not possible to give the king a price tag.

Any values assigned to the other pieces must be regarded as a rough guide. With pawn counting as a basic one unit,
Knight = 3 pawns
bishop = 3 pawns
rook = 5 pawns
queen = 9–10 pawns

These are not hard and fast values; obviously a pawn likely to become a queen has a higher value. Bishops and knights are worth about $3\frac{1}{3}$ pawns early in the game and barely three in the endgame stages.

Parrying Attacks
A knowledge of defensive resources is important to both the attacking player who should reckon with them in his calculations as well as to the defender. We have seen (p. 16) and anew from diagram 53, that checks can be parried by:

1 capturing the checking piece (♘d5xb4)
2 moving off the line of attack (♔e1—e2)
3 interposing a piece (♗c1—d2).

These three ideas apply equally to the defence of situations other than check as in diagram 54 where the black queen (g4) is attacking the rook (d1). White can interpose queen (♕f3) or pawn (f2—f3), but of course the piece thrust into the gap should, if possible, not exceed the value of the attacker; if the attacking piece at g4 was a bishop (instead of the queen), it would be nonsense to interpose the queen. The rook can also be moved.

There are additional resources applicable against attacks other than checks; there is counter-attack against a target of greater or at least equal importance. Diagram 54 is also an example of this; instead of interposing, White can play 1 ♕e3—e7 threatening to take the black rook and, at the same time, mate. This is a counter-attack. In return Black can rid himself of the attack by forcing a queen swap through the check 1 ... ♕g4—e4; after 2 ♕e7xe4 d5xe4 the skirmish has come to an end.

Game

White opened 1 f2—f4 which isn't popular, as it does not immediately help to bring a back-ranker into play—bringing his king out is the very last thing White wants to do at this stage of the game. Black sacrificed a pawn by 1 ... e7—e5 2 f4xe5 d7—d6 3 e5xd6 ♗f8xd6 in order to make his queen and both bishops ready for action. White played 4 ♘b1—c3 which is a good idea to the extent that it's an attempt to bring a piece into play. But it's the wrong move; his king's security problems are missed or ignored; if White had played the other knight (♘g1—f3) the coming disaster would have been averted. Now Black finishes the game with a short violent attack by 4 ... ♕d8—h4+ 5 g2—g3 (diag 55) this is the only way to meet the check, but the barrier is brushed aside by 5 ... ♗d6xg3+ 6 h2xg3 ♕h4xg3 mate.

How to Win

There are three ways for you to win a chess game. You checkmate your opponent. He can resign the game as he sees that checkmate is inevitable, either in the short term or long run, and that you have the necessary experience or knowledge to carry out the winning plan. The third way occurs at expert levels, when you are using the special chess clocks and your opponent fails to make sufficient moves within the fixed time limit. (More about this on p. 23.) In the game, given in the last paragraph, the white player, if he had seen the cunning checkmate, could have resigned with honour and dignity or whatever he resigns with, after 4 . . . ♛h4+.

How do Draws Come About?

Fischer and Spassky, during their historic encounter in 1972, drew 11 of their 21 games. There are four ways of drawing.

The most usual is by agreement. One player asks 'Draw?' and the offer is accepted. The most common reason for this procedure is lack of a mating force left on the board. Two bare kings (diag 56)— hopeless draw. Neither a single bishop (diag 57) nor a lone knight (diag 58) can give check and cover the adjacent square needed to construct a mating net.

A substantiated claim, that the position has happened (or is about to happen) three times, with the same player to move each time, automatically terminates the game. There are many technical points about this particular rule, e.g. the positions need not occur on successive moves. . . . In case of difficulty you should obtain a copy of *The Laws of Chess* from your national chess federation. In diagram 59 the black queen keeps on checking by . . . ♛h4—e1 and . . . ♛e1—h4.

A draw can also be claimed and conceded after both players have made 50 moves during which there has been no capture made nor pawn moved. If a pawn is played on move 49 you start counting all over again.

In both the repetition and 50 move rules, the draw can only be claimed by the player whose turn it is to move. You must not interrupt or distract your opponent during his thinking time.

Stalemate

The fourth and most intriguing way to make a draw is through stalemate. This arises when the player whose turn it is to move and whose king is **not** in check, has *no* move. In diagram 60, the black

king is not in check, and cannot move on to squares covered by the white king (g7, f7 and e7) and the pawn (e8 and g8). Stalemate is the verdict in the queen endings (diags 61 and 62) if it is White to move.

Pieces Active as a Team

What should one be trying to do early in the game? Mate the opponent if the opportunity arises. But there may be no weaknesses along the approaches to his king. Then you will need to battle for lesser advantages and achievements as a stepping stone towards victory.

As a preliminary towards building up an overwhelming array of forces in the vicinity of the enemy king, it's important to bring all your back row pieces into action; all that is, except the king, which must be kept out of harm's way.

Treat your pieces as a team. Place each of them where they are poised and active. Have them marking and restraining the opponent's.

Do not adventure with the queen alone. In the first games given, early forays with the queen brought success, but examine them carefully. In the first example (p. 22) the queen came out prematurely and White's victory was gained by Black's major mistake on his third move, in the second the queen's move gave mate, while in the third the attack with the queen was demonstrably decisive.

Have a look at Spassky's position (diag 63) from a game in the 1973 USSR Championship; he's White. His knights and bishops have left the back rank and taken up posts within reach of the black position; his queen ready to sally further afield; the rooks are stationed on the threshold of the most open files; his king is castled. Spassky's position is nearly ideal; he felt ready to attack; turn to p. 73 to see how the game went.

2 Sets and equipment

Chess sets come in a great variety of forms. Complete chess sets of the pieces used in the very first years of the game in India and Pakistan do not seem to exist. Those were the years when the rulers lived in circumstances of great power and pomp and one should expect sets may have been magnificently ornate in ivory to match the style of living. The British Museum has fragments of pieces found in the ruins of Mansura—about 50 miles NE of Hyderabad—which was destroyed by earthquake in the early 1000s. They were originally of ivory, but have deteriorated to a slightly chalky condition.

From before then, museums all over the world have the odd piece(s).

Arab Sets

Arab sets had to conform to the rigid laws of Islam—no graven image of animal or man. So a lot had to be left to the imagination. Even the symbolism adopted rarely satisfied the holy men. It may be possible to see a faint outline of the horse's features in the sketch. It is easy to see how the chariot or ship for the orient, so represented, had no trouble changing in Europe to a galleon, tower or castle. Probably Arab pieces were made from quartz or bone.

Chess arrived in Europe possibly as early as the 800s and as the centuries went by the faceless Arab pieces slowly changed.

The chess pieces found at Ager in Catalonia, Spain and the Charlemagne chessmen in the Dom, Osnabruck, West Germany still show the influence of the Arab pieces very strongly. H. J. R. Murray in his monumental work *A History of Chess* (Oxford University Press) describes very early European conventional pieces '. . . the Kings and Queens were represented by figures shaped roughly as a throne, the Aufin (Old French for a bishop) and knight by cylindrical figures, the Aufin with two projecting lumps—possibly to represent the elephant's tusks, the knight with one lump to represent the horse's head, the Rook by a narrow rectangular block with a deep depression across the top, and the Pawn by a smaller thimble-shaped piece.'

In Europe the pieces began to represent the structure of society—something very much an issue of those times. The game of war was frowned upon. Something of the morality play was thrown into its composition.

The Lewis Pieces
The Lewis chess set (see photo) is based on 78 pieces that were found on the Isle of Lewis in 1831: 63 are now in the British Museum and 11 in the Scottish National Museum. A Lewis type queen was found independently in County Neath, Ireland, probably in the 1840s. Experts say they were made before AD 1200. The Lewis pieces are magnificently carved. The king has his broadsword. The horses under the knights are small, pony-like. Our castle of today seems to be represented by the guard; if you like simplicity of lines you'll find it the most attractive; the plain shield; the sword at the ready. You can compare this set with the photo of the Leipzig set—it's a replica of one from the 13th century. Look at the ornate carving on the backs. It must have been made for a great king.

The chessmen illustrating the English edition of Cessolis' *The Game and Playe of the Chesse*, are shown next.

This is from the second book to be printed in the English language—by William Caxton at Bruges c. 1474 or 1475. The pieces from left to right are king, queen, bishop, knight, rook and pawn.

Chessmen from Caxton's " Game of Chess."

The rook does not seem to have been represented as a castle until the 1500s.

The next illustration shows a very graceful English regency set that was illustrated in Peter Pratt's then anonymous work, *Studies of Chess*, 1804.

Pre-Staunton Chessmen from " 1804 Studies of Chess."

Staunton Sets

The plate and photo show pieces from a genuine Staunton set; it is the same make as Fischer and Spassky used during their 1972 match at Reykjavik. With some variations the pattern is the only one in use in current international and other serious competitive chess. The pieces are of UK design and manufacture. Nathaniel Cook conceived their form in 1849. It was designed in simple and unmistakable form to counter-act the prevalent refusals to play with pieces of varying shapes, often difficult to distinguish, which were then available.

Cook registered the design, but three years later came to an agreement for the signature of Howard Staunton to appear in facsimile on the boxes, Staunton being the leading English player of the age. Cook's business was taken over by the then Hatton Gardon and now Croydon firm, John Jaques and Son. The firm continues to this day to produce these beautifully proportioned sets. How can one dare make a bad move with such pieces?

Though the handcrafted items are in short supply, there are a number of staunton pattern sets on the market. The photo illustrates a plastic set, manufactured in Hong Kong, with the king $3\frac{3}{4}$ inches high, which is used widely in chess congresses and even in British Championship contents. They are cheap, well-finished; but for long games I wish the white pieces in their ivory sort of shade could be softened even more. The sharp contrast between black and white pieces and also the black and white squares is too hard on the eyes—manufacturers please note.

From the earliest times beautiful chess sets have been fashioned from ivory and some of the most beautiful sets have been created. Photos following show two such sets in that vanishing material. A lovely contemporary set in silver is depicted overleaf. Made by Gerald Benney (Mr. Winter), it won an award in the silversmiths' competition sponsored by the Arts Council and organised by the goldsmiths' company in 1970. Then there is a splendid clear and blue crystal set.

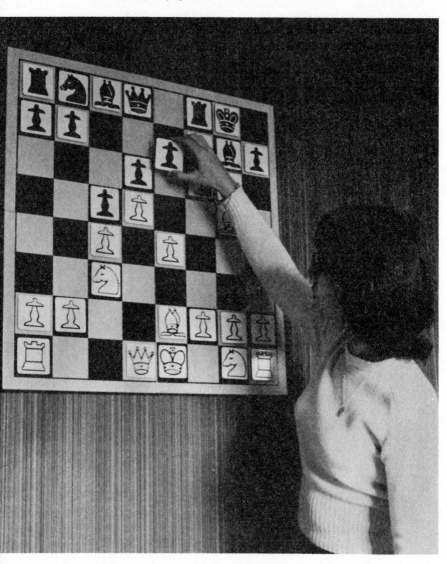

Special vertical demonstration boards have been designed for the benefit of audiences; these are usually magnetic. In addition there is a great variety of pocket and travelling sets in the shops in which magnetic pieces are the commonest components.

Chess Clocks

The photograph shows a special chess clock. It is two clocks within one frame; each player has a separate clock. Chess clocks are constructed so that only one clock can be in motion at any one time;

when the player presses the button above (nearest) his clock, it stops his own clock and starts that of his opponent ticking. The opponent thinks, makes his move and then presses the button nearest him; that stops his clock and, at the same time, starts the other. His clock has recorded the actual time that he spent on the move.

If the game is important the players will usually have agreed to a time limit in which forty moves have to be made in 2 or $2\frac{1}{2}$ hours. The players write down the moves as they are played on a scoresheet. (See p. 20 N.B. The Réti-Alekhine game, recorded on the score-sheet, is one of the finest ever played; it contains what is possibly the longest combinative sequence.) Clocks add both to the tension and excitement of a game. Players often become acutely short of time, so much so that they have to move instantaneously for many moves. What we call a flag, at the top of each clock, is the final arbiter of when the hour is reached. As the hour is approached, the flag is pushed up gradually by the minute hand to a horizontal position; at the moment the hour is reached the flag falls; a player must have made the required number of moves before it falls—failure to do so means the loss of the game.

3 Basis for attack

Among Mates—The Queen

To give checkmate with king and queen against king should be easy. Diagrams 64–68 show the basic mating positions. There are five of them; notice that the black king is needed in all.

If you have to mate with king and queen against lone king, you will have to reach one of those basic positions. The king was driven to the edge of the board in each case. The attacking king was needed to stop the prey escaping away from the edge.

Now for an example of how this is done. Have a look at diagram 69. It's White to play. He should be able to force checkmate in ˈbout 8 moves. That's 7 moves each, and by the next move White shˌ ˈld have given checkmate. Try to work out ways of tackling this endiˌ.g for yourself before reading any further.

But remember not to stalemate the black king. Just avoid the positions in diagrams 61 and 62.

Did you manage to mate in 8 moves? What method did you develop? One of the hallmarks of a master is the precision and economy with which he tackles even the simplest tasks.

This is the way I would set about the queen ending. In all the

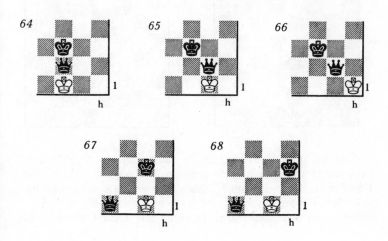

basic positions the king was mated on the edge of the board. There-fore it must first be driven there, and for this both king and queen are needed. I start with 1 ♔f2 , and Black would probably reply 1 . . . ♚f5, trying to stay away from the edges; I still advance my king: 2 ♔f3, and Black naturally stays around the centre: 2 . . . ♚e5. Now that I cannot make progress with my king, I look for the most restricting queen move—3 ♕d7; when Black tries 3 . . . ♚f6 my king can sweep forward again—4 ♔f4. Black has only 4 . . . ♚g6. Again my king cannot advance, so I play another limiting queen move—5 ♕e7. In reply Black should play 5 . . . ♚h6 (the other king move lets White mate in one). Once more the white king can edge closer, 6 ♔f5, there being no stalemate. The black king is left with 6 . . . ♚h5 and White has the choice of two mates—7 ♕h7 or 7 ♕g5.

Did you notice that White's first check with the queen was the one that gave mate? Priority was given to bringing up the slow but necessary king.

Complex Mates

More often than not, however, a game will not reach such a simple ending. From mates with very reduced material, let us see how to pluck mates from the most complicated positions.

First you must be able to recognise the essentials of likely mates—a king checked, with flight squares covered or blocked. We have seen basic mates with king and queen versus king, but it won't happen very often that the king is active in complicated middle-games. More likely partners for the queen are the knight, the bishop and the rook.

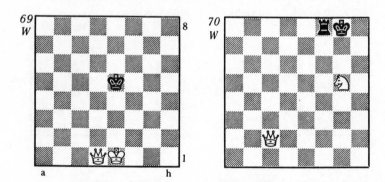

Take the position in diagram 70: White can play 1 ♕h7 mate. Let's merge this into a game position (see diagram 71); it's still 1 ♕h7 mate. But in diagram 72, Black has a knight at f6 covering h7, so if White's queen is played to h7 it can be captured. White needs to eliminate the defending knight: he could play 1 ♘d5! (see diag 73).

This attacks both Black's key defender (the knight on f6) and his queen. Black cannot afford to take: 1 ... ♘xd5 2 ♕h7 mate. He must save the queen, yet if we move it, 1 ... ♕d8, White will play 2 ♘xf6+ and after 2 ... ♕xf6 comes the planned 3 ♕h7 mate.

In diagram 74, it is Black to move. The white king's position has some gaps and possible weaknesses around it. Can Black create mating possibilities? What pieces will have access to the neighbourhood of the target king? What pieces are bearing or can be brought to bear on that area? What basic position is available? Can Black achieve the same end position as in diagram 75? Returning to diagram 74, can the black knight be moved to the same square as in that basic position? Yes, after 1 ... ♘g4, the knight is safe as White's bishop is tied to the diagonal b7—h1 because of the pin. Has White a defence? A king move still allows mate. Nothing can be interposed between the black queen at c7 and the square h2. And there is no counter-threat; White cannot stop the mate.

One is immediately struck by the white-square weaknesses around White's king in diagram 76. Black has a bishop (on d5) overseeing some of those squares (h1, g2, f3). The basic mate position (diag 77) may suggest itself to you. You can super-impose it on your image of the complete position (diag 78). Can it be brought

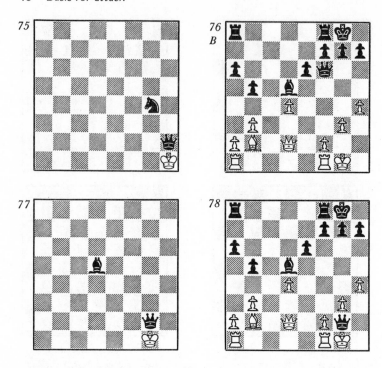

about? The queen joins the bishop's diagonal by **1 . . . ♛f3**, and White has no defence to **1 . . . ♛g2** mate, and only one defence to the alternative **2 . . . ♛h1** mate.

Diagram 79 shows a position that arose in the 1973 Hastings international tournament. White, the Swedish grandmaster, Andersson, played **1 ♛xc7??** He had overlooked the possibility of a bishop mate. What did William Hartston, the 1973 British Champion, who was Black, now play? After **1 . . . ♛h3+!** Andersson resigned. He saw that if **2 ♔h1** there would come **2 . . . ♛f1+   3 ♗g1 ♛xf3** mate, while **2 ♔xh3** leads to the mate by **2 . . . ♗f1!**

You would look to see how to increase your attacking prospects on the king's side if you had the black pieces in diagram 80. Can you imagine the queen and pawn basic mate? See diagram 81! So in the complex position, Black can push the pawn, **1 . . . f3**, which threatens to reach the basic mate. White can only stop it by **2 g3**, but Black can still reach the basic mate. He, with **2 . . . ♛h3**, slips round White's g-pawn; White can no longer postpone the mate.

We are still looking for mates; see diagram 82. Black can check (**1 . . . ♛g4+**) and check (**2 . . . ♛f3+**) and keep on checking with the queen. That would be a draw; to give mate the queen will need

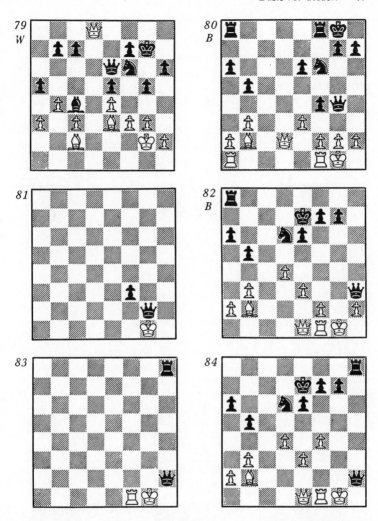

assistance. Which black piece should we choose: the knight or the far-away rook? Which basic mate involves a rook? (Look at diagram 83.) That should suggest the idea of playing **1 ... ♖h8** and, suddenly, White is lost; he cannot stop **2 ... ♛xh2** mate; not even if he moves the f-pawn (see diagram 84).

Rook Mates

From the pevious examples, you could quite correctly deduce that a lot of mates are administered to kings stationed on the edge of the board or in the corner. But the queen is by no means the only piece that inflicts those mates. Here are some basic positions with a rook mating.

Diagram 85 shows the king helping; this is useful to know as it is the position to aim for when mating in the ending king and rook versus king.

The mate with two rooks has already been shown in chapter 1, from diagram 19.

Diagram 86 shows an analogous mate with Black's escape blocked by his own pawns; and a fairly similar position using a queen, with its diagonal coverage, is seen in diagram 87.

Diagram 88 shows the rook supported by the bishop; the rook and knight mate, shown in diagram 89, is called the 'Arabs' mate' from being possible in pre-European chess; the moves of the rook and knight are the only ones to remain unchanged.

In the next basic position (diag 90) the black king has a flight square open (h7) and can escape from the check. Going one step further, diagrams 91, 92, 93 present White controlling the escape square respectively with his bishop, knight and pawn.

Black escapes from the corner in diagram 94 by . . . ♔g7. This escape would not be possible if White had a pawn at f6 (diag 95), bishop at h6 (diag 96), a knight at f5 (diag 97) or a rook at g5 (diag 98).

These by no means cover all the checkmating positions in which a rook is used, but they give a fair range of them. The following two positions give practical examples.

Black, if it was his turn to move, would mate by **1 . . . ♖a4** in diagram 99; but, if it was White's turn, mate can be forced by **1 ♖d8+ ♖xd8 2 ♖xd8.** In the next diagram (100), Black's back row has been strengthened—he has two rooks guarding it; queens have also been added and the white king has an extra pawn (a2) for shelter. Nevertheless, Black, has in essence, the same mate as in the previous position, viz. **1 . . . ♖xa2+!**, removing the White king's cover, **2 ♔xa2 ♕a6.** And have you found the same mate again for White? After the preliminary forced removal of one of the rooks, **1 ♕xb8+! ♖xb8**, Black's back row is again inadequately guarded, and White has **2 ♖d8+ ♖xd8 3 ♖xd8.**

Bishop Mates
Here are some basic bishop mates. In diagram 101 the white king can be played to g1. In diagram 102 this flight square is occupied by his

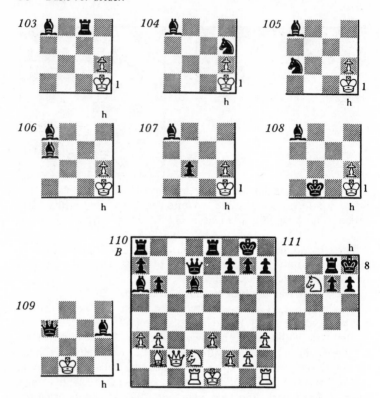

own bishop, while in diagrams 103, 104, 105, 106, 107 and 108 the escape is cut off by a variety of black pieces. The next basic diagram (109) shows a queen and bishop inter-acting to give mate. This idea is carried into the next position (diag 110); if White had no pawn at f2, Black could play . . . ♗g3 mate. How can Black force this mate? Answer: 1 . . . ♖xe3+ 2 f2xe3 ♗g3.

Knight Mates

Kings are most vulnerable to mate when on a corner square as from there they normally have the least number of neighbouring squares to which to flee. Here are four samples. The smothered mate shown in diagram 111 is the most distinctive, the black king being entirely hemmed in by its own men. In the next three (diags 112, 113 and 114) the escape squares are covered by a rook, a queen and by a knight. The next two positions (diags 115 and 116) show a bishop helping the knight. And this provides the lead-in to the following game position (diag 117); the white rook occupies the square needed by the knight to give checkmate; 1 ♖xg6+ is the most forceful way for the rook to be got out of the way; after **1 . . . f7xg6** White mates by **2 ♘h6**.

A Pawn Mate

Pawns can also give mate (diagram 118 is an example) but such happenings are rare.

As an example of play laced stiffly with early checkmates, there is this game published by the Italian, Gioachino Greco, in the early 1600s: **1 e4 e6 2 d4 ♘f6 3 ♗d3 ♘c6 4 ♘f3 ♗e7 5 h4 0–0 6 e5 ♘d5 7 ♗xh7+ ♔xh7 8 ♘g5+**—diagram 119; then Black has five possible replies.

Don't be surprised that, when the king comes forward, it receives rough treatment. If 8 ... ♔h6 then White can uncover check by the bishop (on c1) on to the black king by moving the knight, and would look around for the best way for the knight to inflict damage on to Black's position. Soon he would find that he could win the black queen by double check (9 ♘f7++). And 8 ... ♔g6 could be even worse; there's 9 h5+ ♔f5 10 g4 mate. If 8 ... ♔h8, White mates by 9 ♕h5+ ♔g8 10 ♕h7—one of our basic set-ups.

One of the two serious defences is 8 ... ♔g8; White would play 9 ♕h5 to threaten 10 ♕h7 mate, with the variation 9 ... ♗b4+ 10 c3 ♖e8 11 ♕xf7+ ♔h8 12 ♕h5+ ♔g8 13 ♕h7+ ♔f8 14 ♕h8+ ♔37 15 ♕xg7 mate. The other serious defence occured in the file 9 h4xg5+ and after 9 ... ♔g8, White, by 10 ♕h5 has a mate in the offing (11 ♕h8—queen supported by rook). By 10 ... f5, Black opened an escape route, which White plugged with 11 g6. Black played 11 ... ♖e8 and White mated 12 ♕h8.

One more game: 1 e4 e5 2 ♘f3 d6 3 ♗c4 ♗g4 4 ♘c3 White is bringing his men into action quickly. 4 ... h6? This is bad because it doesn't help to develop his pieces. White can now win a pawn. 5 ♘xe5! White offers his queen as he has a mate in mind. 5 ... ♗xd1? Comparatively best for Black is to take the knight and allow White to take the bishop. 6 ♗xf7+ ♔e7 7 ♘d5 checkmate. This is known as Légal's Mate, after a French player of two hundred years ago. For a change the king is neither on the edge nor in the corner of the board.

Tactical Weapons
You should store in your memory some hint of every tactical device remotely likely. Without such a fund of ideas, based on the collective skill of generations of players, it is possible to stare at the chessboard for a long time, and still not see an otherwise obvious solution to the problems of the position.

The first branch of tactics is devoted to forms of double attacks; exploiting positions where one move attacks two targets simultaneously. The simplest form is the fork, which can be carried out by any piece or pawn.

Forks
Diagram 120 illustrates a knight fork—the white knight is attacking both the black king and rook; the king moves and then White may take the rook.

In diagram 121 we see the knight forking king and queen. Can you transfer this idea to the position in diagram 122, in which it's Black to move? Black obtained a winning material advantage with 1 ... ♗xf2+. The bishop is forking the white king and queen. If

120

121

122
B

2 ♔xf2, Black again forks king and queen, by 2 . . . ♘xe4+; and if
2 ♕xf2 then 2 . . . ♘d3+; in both cases White loses his queen.

The following short game was won by Jonathan Penrose, who was
British champion ten times during the twelve year period 1958 to
1969; he was Black. **1 d4 ♘f6 2 c4 e6 3 ♘f3 d5 4 g3 dc 5 ♘bd2
c5 6 dc** White is playing too passively. **6 . . . ♗xc5 7 ♗g2**. Now
Penrose initiated a decisive attack based on knight forks. **7 . . .
♗xf2+ 8 ♔xf2 ♘g4+** (diag 123). This check leaves White three
possibilities. If **9 ♔f1** Black has the knight fork **9 . . . ♘e3+**. If **9 ♔g1**
Black forces mate with **9 . . . ♕b6+**. White played **9 ♔e1** but resigned
after Penrose's reply—**9 . . . ♘e3**; his queen is lost. If **10 ♕a4+** then
10 . . . ♗d7 forces either **11 ♕a3** or **11 ♕b4**, and in both cases Black
has **11 . . . ♘c2+** and captures the queen next move.

The position in diagram 124 illustrates one of the most common

123
W

124
B

types of bishop fork: after Black plays **1** . . . ♘xc3, if White recaptures, **2 bc**, Black, by **2** . . . ♗xc3+, forks king and rook.

Diagram 125 shows the two-pronged possibilities of a king journey. It is Black to move; he needs to stop White's a-pawn from queening on a8, and he can win it by a direct approach (1 . . . ♔b3) and take it on his next move. In the meantime, however, the white king would be winning Black's remaining pawn and preparing to promote his own e-pawn. White would then win; but in fact, by a little ingenuity, Black can turn the tables. His king takes six moves to reach a8—sufficient to stop White's a-pawn whether it travels via b3–b4–b5–b6–b7–a8 or d3–e4–d5–c6–b7–a8; therefore Black can remove both white pawns by the second journey, and win! After 1 ... ♔d3! White can try two plans, but they both fail:

a) 2 a4 ♔xe4 3 a5 ♔d5 4 a6 ♔c6 5 a7 ♔b7 6 a8=♕+ ♔xa8 or

b) 2 ♔g7 ♔xe4 3 ♔f6 ♔d4 4 ♔f5 e4 5 ♔f4 e3 6 ♔f3 ♔d3 and Black is winning.

I would like to illustrate a pawn fork by these opening moves: 1 e4 e5 2 ♘c3 ♘f6 3 ♗c4. Now Black can soundly and usefully play 3 ... ♘xe4 as after the recapture, 4 ♘xe4, Black has the pawn fork 4 ... d5 regaining his piece. At the same time, Black is bringing forces—particularly the bishop on c8—into play with increased momentum.

With the aid of forking possibilities by his rook, White can win Black's bishop in the position in diagram 126. After 1 ♔c3, the bishop can move to any one of four squares where it cannot be captured, or, as we say, is not en prise. But White can organise a rook fork in each case: if 1 ... ♗a2 or 1 ... ♗a4 then 2 ♖a6+; if 1 ... ♗g8, White plays 2 ♖d8+. It takes one move longer if Black plays 1 ... ♗f7. White has to check first by 2 ♖d8+ and then, after 2 ... ♔b7 or 2 ... ♔a7, 3 ♖d7+ wins the bishop.

125
B

126
W

In diagram 127 the queen fork is one move away. White must eliminate the knight by 1 ♗xf6 and, after either recapture, continue 2 ♕e4, threatening both mate at h7 and, on the other side, the doomed rook on a8.

Pins and Skewers
Other forms of double attack can be against two pieces on the same line. These attacks can be of two kinds, pins and skewers.

Diagram 128 illustrates the pin. The white queen is pinned to the file; the attempt to move it off the line would expose a more valuable piece, the king, to capture by the black rook. Also, as a further example, the white knight is tied to the diagonal since it is shielding the king from capture.

The other type of double attack along the same line is the skewer, illustrated by diagram 129. In this, a piece is driven off a line, leaving a second piece exposed. Here the white queen is skewering the black king and queen. In diagram 130 the bishop skewers king and rook, while the rook skewers bishop and knight in diagram 131.

The position in diagram 132 is a particularly good example of exploiting a pin. White plays **1 ☖xb7** as, after the black rook recaptures, **1 . . . ☖xb7**, it is tied to the diagonal and cannot move, at least for the moment. This gives White the opportunity to play his pawn up, **2 a6**, attacking the rook for a second time, and after **2 . . . ☗b8**, take the rook with the pawn.

Without a skewer, the ending in diagram 133 would be difficult
to win. With a fine temporary sacrifice of his queen, 1 ♕h2+, forcing
1 . . . ♕xh2, White reaches an ending, which after 2 b8=♕+ ♔ moves
and 3 ♕xh2, should be a matter of technique.

Ambushes

The next class of tactical manoeuvre is the ambushes. This is the
form they take: a piece is moved, usually with a threat, uncovering
a second piece, which either gives check or has some other separate
threat. In diagram 134 White, by moving the bishop, uncovers his
rook, which thus gives check to Black's king. To make the move
more effective, White plays 1 ♗g5++ or 1 ♗f2+, attacking the black
queen and king.

There have been a lot of novices' games that have opened 1 e4 e5
2 ♘f3 ♘f6 3 ♘xe5 (diag 135) 3 . . . ♘xe4? (It is better to play
3 . . . d6 first, pushing back the knight.) 4 ♕e2 ♘f6? This loses the
queen to 5 ♘c6+ discovering check from the white queen and
attacking the black queen.

White has a very neat example of a discovered attack in the composed position in diagram 136. By 1 ♔b3, attacking the black rook,

133
W

134
W

135
B

136
W

White also opens the file for his rook, and threatens 2 ⬛c1 mate. Black must lose the rook.

In diagram 137, the masking piece moves and gives check, 1 ⬛a2+, opening the diagonal of the bishop.

A sample from actual play is **1 e4 c5 2 ♘f3 d6 3 d4 cd 4 ♘xd4 ♘f6 5 ♘c3 g6 6 f4 ♗g7 7 e5 de 8 fe ♘g4**—not best—**9 ♗b5+ ♔f8** and now White should play **10 ♘e6+**, uncovering the white queen on to Black's.

Over-Extended

This complex class of tactical manoeuvres includes deflecting and destroying guards and exploiting overworked pieces. They are related. In diagram 138 a simple example of a guard being forcibly deflected has arisen. The black rook has the all-important job of stopping the white pawn from queening, therefore it must not leave the c-file. But it cannot cope with White's move **1 ⬛d4**, pinning it along the rank. After **1 . . . ⬛xd4** White queens the pawn. Queen and king should normally win against rook and king!

137 W

138 W

139 B

When you examine the position in diagram 139, you will find that White's knight has the important role of guarding the g-pawn and stopping Black from giving mate. Black gets rid of the guard by playing **1 . . . ☐xe3** and White has neither time to re-take nor to defend his rook.

By checking the functions of the black pieces in diagram 140, we will find that Black's rook has two jobs, namely—to protect the pawn at f7, which White is attacking with queen and bishop, and to protect his queen. When it is forced to deal with **1 ♗xf7+** by capturing the bishop, it is no longer available to carry out its other duty, so after **1 . . . ☐xf7** White wins by **2 ♕xd8+**.

We'll take leave of this group with the position in diagram 141, in which a light deflection is nonetheless decisive. If White advances, **1 a6**, Black can stop it by **1 . . . ♗e3** placing his bishop on to the g1—a7 diagonal. The pawn will only be advanced further over the bishop's dead body, Black being willing to give up the bishop for the pawn if necessary, as the draw would then be certain; his king can cope with the g-pawn. White must stop the bishop getting on the g1—a7 diagonal. But how? If **1 ♔e4** Black plays **1 . . . ♗f8**, threatening to join the diagonal at c5. White must drive the bishop on to an inferior diagonal by the pawn sacrifice **1 g5+**. After **1 . . . ♔xg5** the black king has got in the way of the bishop, and White can happily push the pawn on to queen—**2 a6, 3 a7** and **4 a8=♕**. And what if **1 . . . ♗xg5**, the only reasonable alternative? Then **2 ♔e4**, and once more the black king obstructs its own bishop. The only chance it has of reaching the important 17—g1 diagonal in two moves is by **2 . . . ♗h4**, but when White puts paid to all tries with **3 ♔f3**, Black can resign. The pawn cannot be stopped.

Sabotage

The next grouping would seem to be an anarchist's dream—the creation of traffic jams and obstructions! Usually these are evolved from simple interpositions.

Diagram 142 demonstrates an example of successful interposition. White would like to queen the pawn without giving Black the chance to exchange his rook for it. He can bring the knight to c8, shutting out Black's rook by aid of **1 ♘e7+**, and after the king moves, White's knight interposes (**2 ♘c8**) and his pawn should queen next move.

With the position in diagram 143, we graduate to downright obstructiveness. White wants to push his sole remaining pawn home to queen, but, if 1 a7, Black easily stops it with the diagonal-opener **1 . . . d4**, after which White has no hope of advancing the pawn and keeping the queen. Yet by playing first **1 ♗d4**, White ensures that the diagonal is blocked for at least three moves.

It was the Estonian grandmaster, Paul Keres, who constructed the obstacle course in diagram 144. White, with only king and bishop, has to play and mate the black king in four moves. It's done by inducing Black to get his pieces hopelessly entangled. After **1 ♗d2**, Black stops mate by **1 . . . ♖c7**. If instead, the bishop had gone to e3, 1 . . . ♖d7 would have kept the bishop out of the crucial a1–h8 diagonal, while, if 1 ♗f4, then 1 . . . ♘f7 holds up the bishop. The solution is **1 ♗g5!** threatening **2 ♗f6**, and after **1 . . . ♖f7** (necessary), the knight can no longer go to that square. Now **2 ♗f4** forces **2 . . . ♘c6** where it blocks the c-file, and only now **3 ♗d2**, as no black piece can reach the c3 square to prevent mate next move.

Diagram 145 embodies an open/shut manoeuvre. Black by **1 . . .**

b3 opens the diagonal for his queen to go to e1, shuts White's queen out from the defence of a2, and incidentally threatens 2 . . . ♛xa2 mate! White has no good defence.

A particularly flamboyant example of obstruction or line interference occurs in diagram 146. Examining the roles of the black pieces we find that the bishop, besides attacking the white rook, is stopping the white a-pawn queening at a8, while the black rook is stopping the other white pawn on e7. The routes for the two black pieces intersect at d5. White therefore parks his rook on this junction square—1 ♖d5!! If the bishop takes, the rook is blocked, and White queens the d-pawn with check (1 . . . ♝xd5 5 d8=♛+); if rook takes (1 . . . ♖xd5), the a-pawn queens (2 a8=♛). The experts call this a Nowotny Interference. It's a rarity, but nevertheless revealing.

Clearances
The opposite of obstructions are the vacating of squares and the clearance of lines.

In diagram 147, Black's bishop on f2 occupies the square which Black would like to be free for his knight to go to and fork White's king, queen and rook. If he looks around for the most effective bishop move, he will quite likely to come up with 1 . . . ♝xg3! etc.

There are various ways of clearing lines. The example in diagram 148, was specially composed to illustrate the *Bristol clearance*. White vacates the queening square for his pawn and clears most of the diagonal by 1 ♝g2; Black follows similar reasoning with his long bishop move, 1 . . . ♝h8. Play would continue with mutual pawn promotions 2 a8=♛ a1=♛. Now with queen following its bishop right down the diagonal, 3 ♛f3, White threatens mate by 4 ♛g4. Black stops it by the Bristolian move 3 . . . ♛g7, but now White moves 4 ♝f1, planning 5 ♝e2, with 6 ♛f2 or 6 ♛e1, mating, to follow. After 4 . . . ♛g6, white first plays 5 ♝d3.

Forcing Moves

From clearing the arteries I move on to forcing sequences like
checks, the attack of a weaker unit on to a more powerful one, mate
theats and so on, and to sandwich moves—those interpolations which
can suddenly alter the nature of a position. Vacating squares can be
one aspect of a sandwich move. In diagram 149 the black knight is
forking the two white rooks but White escapes with 1 ♖e8+, and
after 1 . . . ♔h7 moves his other rook out of danger.

Like all other moves, checks should be played with a purpose.
Don't check for the sake of checking! Do you remember the queen
and king versus king ending two chapters ago? Plenty of checks
available, but none were given—until mate. In our next position
(diag 150) White has plenty of checks, each one drawing the net
tighter around the black king. They go 1 ♕g7+, 2 ♕f7+, 3 ♕f6+ and
the white queen continues checking down the staircase (4 ♕e6+,
5 ♕e5+, 6 ♕d5+, 7 ♕d4+, 8 ♕c4+, 9 ♕c3+, 10 ♕b3+) with the black
king monotonously alternating between a2 and a1. Eventually
White mates by 11 ♕xa3.

Diagram 151 contains a fine example of a sandwich move (or an
in-between move, or an intermediate move) or the German form

used among many expert players—the *zwischenzug*. If White takes
the rook straight away (1 ♕xa8) Black has the adequate reply of
1 . . . ♕xe5+ and will be in no danger of losing. But White has the
sandwich move 1 ♕f3+ forcing Black's king back either to e8 or g8,
when White can take the rook with check (2 ♕xa8+) and thus remain with an extra bishop.

The 'desperado' combination is part of the sandwich move scene.
Consider the sequence 1 e4 e5 2 ♘f3 ♘c6 3 ♘c3 ♘f6 4 d4 ed 5
♘xd4. If a piece is going to be lost next move or so, one looks
around for the most advantageous way of selling it. In this game
Black's next move, 5 . . . ♘xe4?! (diag 152), is based on the pin
6 ♘xe4? ♕e7, as Black has on White's 7 ♘xc6 the sandwich 7 . . .
♕xe4+, coming out a pawn up. Instead the game could go 6 ♘xc6!
and now the series of desperado moves: 6 . . . ♘xc3 7 ♘xd8 ♘xd1
8 ♘xf7 ♘xf2 9 ♘xh8 ♘xh1 and the game continues 10 ♗e3! with
chances for both players. This fantastic sequence of combinations
actually occurred in a 1949 West German championship game.

Promotion

The promotion of a pawn must be regarded as one of the best ways
of gaining a material advantage. Take the confrontation here of three
pawns against three (diag 153). It is White to move. Can he organise
a break-through? Seemingly not, but perhaps he can create a gap?
After 1 b6! Black takes with either his a- or c-pawn; which, is of no
importance here, so we'll play 1 . . . ab. Now, if Black had no pawn
on b7, the white a-pawn would sail through; the b7 pawn is diverted
by the second sacrifice 2 c6—threatening 3 cb and queening on the
following move. Therefore 2 . . . bc 3 a6 and White queens long
before one of Black's pawns can do.

The difference in value between a pawn and a queen is the
incentive for all sorts of ingenuity in getting a pawn home. In the
position in diagram 154, the black knight is forcibly deflected to a

poor square by White's surprise 1 ♘g7+; after 1 . . . ♘xg7 comes 2 h6 and Black cannot stop the pawn going on to h8.

Promoting to a lesser piece than the queen is called 'under-promotion'. Sometimes there can be a reason for under-promoting. We might make a rook or bishop when, by promoting to a queen, we would have brought about a draw by stalemate. We can under-promote to a knight because that piece can go to or cover squares that the queen cannot. One under-promotion idea is shown by diagram 155 (something like what happened in one of the games played by the then world champion, Emanuel Lasker, in 1920!). White plays the astonishing 1 ♕a7+! as after 1 . . . ♔xa7, the pawn takes the rook and is promoted to a knight, 2 b7xa8=♘+!, forking king and queen.

Nets

Besides nets woven to mate the king, ways of netting all the other pieces have to be looked out for. Here in diagram 156 the knight traps the rook in the corner (White threatens ♘xa8). In the next position (diag 157), White's bishop is trapped after 1 . . . b5 2 ♗b3 c4 etc. This has happened to chess novices from time immemorial: hence its popular name, the Noah's Ark Trap! In diagram 158 Black's knight has nowhere safe to go and White can win it by 1 g4.

Pieces lying loose (i.e. unprotected) around the board can be a target. In diagram 159 the black rook comes into that category; and White can win it after a series of checks, with the black king having to dodge mates, by **1 ♕d5+ ♚b1 2 ♕e4+ ♚a1** or **2 . . . ♚a2 3 ♕a8+ ♚b1 4 ♕b8+.**

Forcing a Draw

Besides combinations to augment one's material, tactics can be invoked with the aim of drawing the game. These can involve stalemate, or perpetual checking, or in whittling down material to below what is required to give mate.

We've seen queen and king versus king stalemates and an important one from a pawn ending (diag 160). Take the further position in diagram 161; White to move went **1 ♚f8?** and Black sneaked a draw by **1 . . . ♖f7+** as **2 ♚xf7** leaves the black king stalemated.

Of course, stalemate cannot be involved in the position in diagram 162. White has lost his queen, but all the other important pieces are still on the board; White has king, two bishops, two knights, one rook and two pawns able to move. Yet White can force Black to stalemate him! After the bishop check, 1 ♗h2+, Black must take, 1 . . . ♖xh2, and then after 2 ♘e2++ ♚xf5 White, still with six knight moves, three pawn moves and two moves by the bishop, turns them all into statues by 3 g4+ ♚e6 and, lo and behold, stalemate!

Perpetual check is a common way of forcing a draw. Here are some basic positions. In the first (diag 163), the queen goes back and forth—♕g6 and ♕h6; diagram 164 contains a similar theme— 1 ♕f7+ ♚h8 2 ♕f8+ ♚h7 3 ♕f7+ and so on; diagram 165, with ♕h5 and ♕e8, often occurs. The fourth example of this theme (diag 166) could continue 1 ♕f5+ ♚g8 2 ♕c8+ etc., or break down to a simpler one after 1 ♕f5+ g6 and now 2 ♕xf7+ ♚h8 3 ♕f8+ ♚h7 4 ♕f7+ and so on for ever, or rather for three times, when the draw can be claimed.

162
W

163
W

164
W

Repetition of position is the last factor that I want to look at. Diagram 167 is a position from the 11th game between Spassky, (White), and Fischer, in their 1972 match. Spassky now played the knight retreat, 1 ♘b1, attacking Fischer's queen. Fischer could have played 1 . . . ♕b2 when it seems Spassky would come into difficulties if he did not repeat the position by 2 ♘c3; Fischer would have to go back with his queen 2 . . . ♕a3, since the threat would be 3 a3 followed by 4 ♖a2 trapping the black queen. Instead Fischer went 1 . . . ♕b4—to avoid the possible draw—and so got into trouble and lost.

Attacking the King
Attack may be the best defence, but attacks need a basis: some

forces available, some avenues of approach, some weaknesses as targets.

The easiest target is a king. The aim of the attacker will be to build up an overwhelming preponderance of force in the neighbourhood of the opponent's king, and also to destroy or lure away potential defenders.

Alexander Alekhine, the world champion and one of the two finest attacking players of this century, had the white pieces in the position in diagram 168 taken from a 1941 game. All his pieces, except the king rook, are poised for some action on the king-side. He sought out and found the most exact, and really crushing, finish: 1 ♕g6! Black can take with two different pawns: the f- and h-pawns.

White threatens 2 ♕xg7 mate. Bar taking the white queen, the only defence is 1 . . . ♖g8, when White can mate by 2 ♕xh7+, forcing open the h-file; after 2 . . . ♔xh7, 3 ♖h3 is mate. It follows that when Black captures the white queen with his h-pawn, 1 . . . h7xg6, the rook move again mates (2 ♖h3). In both these cases, the black king's flight square, g8, is covered by the white knight on e7. That leaves only the other pawn capture, 1 . . . f7xg6, but White can still force open the h-line by the knight sacrifice 2 ♘xg6+. Black's king still cannot flee, as the white bishop on c4 has taken over the role of covering g8; after 2 . . . h7xg6, once more, we have 3 ♖h3 mate.

The easiest of targets should be the king lacking defensive covering forces. With both kings wide open in diagram 169, the result depends on which player has the move. Black, to move, would just play 1 . . . ☐a1 mate. White, if he had the move, would be able to achieve a similar mating set-up, after systematically driving the black king back to the edge. The method is ♕e2+ ♚f4 2 ☐g4+ ♚f5 then another left hook from the queen—3 ♕e4+—forcing 3 . . . ♚f6, now a right jab 4 ☐g6+, 4 . . . ♚f7, a left 5 ♕e6+. The king is against the ropes, 5 . . . ♚f8, and the right—6 ☐g8—administers mate.

In our diagram 170, Black would like queens to be exchanged. That would leave him a comfortable material advantage, without the present uncertainty stemming from the fact that Black's main forces (queen and rook), are situated on the queen side and may not be adequately supporting the defence of his king. White to move, however, would reject 1 ♕xc6?, and possibly investigate the line 1 ♕xh7+ ♚f8 2 ♕h8+ ♚e7 3 ♕e5+; this would not make him very happy. Then, if he checked the other variation, 1 ♗xh7+ ♚h8, he would find that, with care, he can force mate by 2 ♗g6+ (discovered check from the queen, with the bishop carefully placed to shut off Black's queen) 2 . . . ♚g8 3 ♕h7+ ♚f8 4 ♕xf7 and that's that.

Smothered Mate
Diagram 171 shows a good example of queen and knight co-operation.

They attack together; first comes 1 . . . ♛c5+. The White king has to move, not 2 ♔f1 because of 2 . . . ♛f2 mate, but instead 2 ♔h1. Then, however, 2 . . . ♞f2+ 3 ♔g1 ♞h3++ (why this square, will be explained shortly) 4 ♔h1 and now Black can force a smothered mate. (The ensuing two-move idea has a name—Philidor's Legacy.) Black starts by sacrificing his queen (4 . . . ♛g1+)—the knight was manoeuvred to h3 in order to make it impossible for White to capture the queen with his king—and after 5 ♖xg1 ♞f2 mates.

King in the Middle

The position in diagram 172 represents another type of attack. The king is caught uncastled, and exposed to attack along open central files. After 1 ♖e1+ ♗e7, White can build up on the pinned bishop by 2 ♞d5 while Black can add no more to its protection. His knight is pinned on the b5—e8 diagonal and therefore cannot be interposed at e5. Finally a counter-attack by 2 . . . c6 is too slow: White could continue 3 ♞xe7 c6xb5 4 ♞c6+ (discovered check from the rook) and the black queen is lost.

Into the Breach

Except for the Alekhine position, the four we have shown represent one level at which attacking ideas need to be studied. Now we must progress to a more advanced stage.

One form of successful attack may involve a breaching of the enemy king's fortress, when one has pieces at hand ready to rush in. In diagram 173, the breaching is effected by a sacrifice of one of White's bishops: 1 ♗xh7+. After 1 . . . ♔xh7 White has both queen and rook ready to follow in by 2 ♛h5+ ♔g8 3 ♖h3, with the threat of ♛h7 or ♛h8 mate. The only escape for Black's king is via f7 after Black has played 3 . . . f6 (or 3 . . . f5) when White can plug the gap by 4 e6, after which mate will be unavoidable.

An example of a more thorough breaching of the king's position is diagram 174 taken from the 1973 USSR championship. Black

172
W

173
W

played 1 . . . ♘xb6 which means that this knight, momentarily at least, is not available for defence on the king's wing. Gennady Kuzmin, a Soviet grand master, didn't bother to recapture, but went for a thorough smash by 2 ♗xh7+ ♚xh7 3 ♕h5+ ♚g8 4 ♗xg7 sacrificing a second bishop (diag 175). He threatens mate on h8, and to ignore the bishop and play 4 . . . f6 allows 5 ♕g6 which would clearly be fatal. So Kuzmin's opponent took the bishop, 4 . . . ♚xg7, and the game was concluded by 5 ♕g4+ ♚h7 6 ♖f3 which threatens to mate after 7 ♖h3+. Black's only way to avoid immediate mate is to play 6 . . . ♕d8, giving up the queen (after 7 ♖h3+ ♗h4 8 ♖xh4+ ♕xh4 9 ♕xh4) when, besides a material disadvantage, his pieces would be poorly mobilised. Black preferred to regard the game as hopeless and resigned it.

174
B

175
B

King Hunt

Diagram 176 gives a relatively modest finish by the great German attacking player of the nineteenth century, Adolf Anderssen. It's a queen and rook finale after the initial sacrifice of rook for bishop (1 ♖xb6+ a7xb6 2 ♕xb6+ ♚a8). Now White cannot mate immediately by 3 ♖a1+, because the black queen would take it. Instead, after 3 ♕a6+ ♚b8 4 ♖b1+, Black had to resign. He could see that after 4 . . . ♚c7 5 ♖b7+ ♚c8 (or ♚d8) 6 ♕a8 he would be mated.

A 'king hunt' is a prosaic description of what happens to the black king in the game now to be played through! Perhaps a chess kidnapping, or something sucked out of a quiet chess backyard by a passing tornado, are more appropriate thoughts? It happened in a London club back in 1912. A visiting American engineer, Edward Lasker, had White. 1 d4 f5 2 e4. He gave up a pawn to speed development of his pieces. 2 . . . fe 3 ♘c3 ♘f6 4 ♗g5 e6. This was rather tame. 5 ♘xe4 ♗e7 6 ♗xf6 ♗xf6 7 ♘f3 b6 8 ♗d3 ♗b7 9 ♘e5 Prepared to play 9 ♕h5+ now that the knights and bishop would be ready to co-operate. Black tried 9 . . . 0—0 but White still

176
W

replied **10 ♕h5**. White wanted to move the knight on e4, anywhere, so as to line up his bishop, as well as the queen, on the h7 pawn. Lasker's opponent played **10 . . . ♕e7**, meeting one possibility—now if White played **11 ♘xf6+** Black could reply by **11 . . . g7xf6** and have his queen covering h7. But now the tornado struck, picked up the black king and deposited it on White's back row. **11 ♕xh7+!** Lasker began by giving up his queen, and after **11 . . . ♚xh7** played **12 ♘xf6++**. Double check! Black had to play **12 . . . ♚h6** as after **12 . . . ♚h8   13 ♘g6** would have been checkmate! (diag 177) **13 ♘eg4+ ♚g5   14 h4+ ♚f4   15 g3+ ♚f3** Every white move was check and every reply of Black's was forced. **16 ♗e2+ ♚g2   17 ♖h2+ ♚g1** Made it! But there's no reward (diag 178). **18 ♚d2** That's it—check-

177
W

178
W

mate. 18 0–0–0 is also mate. White missed two opportunities of checkmating in one move less, but, somehow here it doesn't seem to be a flaw. A fantastic game.

Diagram 179 shows a position taken from the 'Evergreen Game' between Anderssen and Dufresne. Anderssen, on whose prowess as an attacking wizard of the last century I have already commented, had the white pieces. The black king has remained uncastled, in the centre. Anderssen's opponent was relying on his threats to the white king—in particular he is ready to play . . . ♛xg2 mate.

Anderssen started his final attack with 1 ♖xe7+ to which his opponent replied with 1 . . . ♞xe7, apparently bringing to an end White's aggressive intentions. But Anderssen had in store the stunning queen sacrifice, 2 ♛xd7+!! and Black must take back, since if 2 . . . ♚f8 3 ♛xe7 is mate. So, 2 . . . ♚xd7 when 3 ♗f5++ followed, and as it is double check, the king must move; if 3 . . . ♚c6, White has 4 ♗d7 mate; Anderssen's opponent played 3 . . . ♚e8, but now White's two bishops co-operate in a mate by 4 ♗d7+ ♚f8 (The same happens if it is played to the other square). 5 ♗xe7 checkmate. That brilliancy was played in Berlin in 1852! This is one advantage that chess possesses, over all other games. Chess games can be written down, and indeed the moves of practically all important games of the last hundred years are available. There are literally thousands of books on chess; and this means we can still learn something from past generations. Our technique, today, may be superior, to that of players of the past, but our games have been immeasurably enriched by the ideas that we have culled from the great players who have gone before us. Bobby Fischer spent time studying and writing about the 19th century greats.

Genius of Attack

The genius of attack in contemporary chess is the Latvian ex-world champion, Mikhail Tal. I would like to show you how he dealt with a complicated position when he was only twelve years old. Look at diagram 180, where Tal had the white pieces. He boldly played

179 W

180 W

1 ♖f6!, where it could be taken by two of Black's pieces! His opponent feared the worst and didn't take it. The game continued 1 . . . ♕f8 2 ♖f4 ♗d7 3 ♘g4 ♗e8 4 ♘f6+ (Tal is determined that Black should not play 4 . . . f5 to improve his internal communications). 4 . . . ♘xf6 5 ef ♖c7 6 fg♔xg7 7 ♕e5+; thus Tal won the rook and the game.

What if Tal's opponent had accepted the rook sacrifice? After 1 . . . gf 2 ef ♘xf6 3 ♕xh6 ♘e4 4 ♗xe4 de 5 ♘d4 Tal would be threatening 6 ♘xf6+, forking king and queen, as well as mate. Black would not defend himself against both. The game would not yet be over, but White would have the better prospects.

This is the sort of ability that we have to measure our 12- and 13-year-olds against, in assessing their potential for international honours and opportunities. By the age of 23 Tal had won the world championship!

Spassky Attacks

Boris Spassky played the following incisive game against Naum Rashkovsky, when winning the 1973 USSR title. Boris was White.

The opening moves were 1 e2–e4 c7–c5 2 ♘g1–f3 d7–d6 3 d2–d4 c5xd4 4 ♘f3xd4 ♘g8–f6 5 ♘b1–c3 a7–a6 (Fischer's favourite defence) 6 ♗c1–g5 e7–e6 7 f2–f4 ♕d8–c7 8 ♗f1–d3 ♘b8–d7 9 ♕d1–e2 b7–b5 10 0–0–0 ♗c8–b7 11 ♖h1–e1 ♗f8–e7. Boris has taken only 4 minutes of his allocated 2½ hours for 40 moves, while on his opponent's clock 6 minutes have elapsed. This position is shown in diagram 63. After one minute's thought, Spassky pushed 12 e4–e5 and three minutes later Rashkovsky answered by 12 . . . d6xe5; after two more minutes Spassky retook—13 f4xe5; he is trying to force open all the approach lines to Black's king at e8. Naum thought for 41 minutes and played the quite aggressive knight move 13 . . . ♘f6–d5 (diag 181).

For his 14th move Spassky pondered for 46 minutes between the move he played and 14 ♘xe6 and settled for 14 ♗g5xe7; he would have gone deeply into his following move as well. When, after 5 minutes, Naum took the knight, 14 ♘d5xc3, Boris took a further 7 minutes before embarking on the all-out attack with 15 ♕e2–g4. There are many sacrificial lines to be calculated. The long thought by both players has determined the character of the struggle ahead.

The question was 'Who's judgement was right?' I remember a penetrating remark of Fischer's, made a decade ago, to the effect that Spassky was able to sacrifice with complete abandon. This is an example. Boris feels that the black king's insecurity will compensate him for any material losses.

25 minutes later Naum Rashkovsky took the rook—15 . . . ♘c3xd1. Now Boris let the time slip by while he worked out the

precise method of attack. It was another 30 minutes on his clock before he played **16 ♘d4xe6** (diag 182); 16 ♗d6 is possibly more accurate, e.g. 16 . . . ♕a5 17 ♕g5 ♕d8 18 ♕xg7. Naum took 45 minutes to reply with **16 . . . ♕c7–c6**; it would have been better to take the knight; he now only had 25 minutes left for 24 moves. Boris spent 27 minutes over **17 ♘e6xg7+**; but now he saw his way through to the end.

Boris's move must have come as a surprise to Naum; although his reply is forced it was 12 minutes before he played **17 . . . ♚e8xe7**; perhaps the thought of impending defeat was having its impact. Boris took five minutes before playing **18 ♕g4–g5+**, met, after a minute's thought, by **18 . . . f7–f6**. Spassky's **19 e5xf6+** took him less than a minute; Naum's clock went on for another 4 minutes before he played **19 . . . ♚e7–d8**; again less than a minute before Spassky checked, **10 f6–f7+**; a further 4 minutes. . . . Rashkovsky moved **20 . . . ♚d8–c7**; another minute, and Spassky checked **21 ♕g5–f4+**. Rashkovsky stared hard at the position; his queen is lost after 21 . . . ♕d6 22 ♘e6+ ♚c6 23 ♗e4; the position is hopeless, and he has 20 moves to find in a minute or two. He knocked over his king—a quite normal procedure—as a token of his resignation.

4 Positional play

Aims of Play

It is appropriate at this stage to issue a general directive of aims for playing a game. I would summarise my approach in the following list:

1 To mate the opposing king;
2 To build up a decisive concentration of pieces on the approaches to the king;
3 To gain an advantage in material that, in time, can be converted into a mating force;
4 To make my pieces work effectively as units and harmoniously as a team;
5 To render the opponent's pieces ineffective;
6 To frustrate the opponent's plans;
7 To draw, if to win is out of the question;
8 Not to lose;
9 If losing, to create chances for the opponent to go wrong;
10 To fight like hell to achieve these objectives;
11 To remain courteous to my opponent.

Pawns—The Soul

Pawns are the soul of chess. So said André Philidor, the dominant French player of two centuries ago. And what he learnt from the writings (1560–1580?) of the Spanish priest, Ruy Lopez, and added to them, has strongly influenced modern play. His games were distinguished through effective cramping by his pawns. The following examples will give some indications of how pawn structures influence piece play.

Pawn Centres

Pawns at e4 and d4 form one typical centre (diag 183); they create a minefield (c5/d5/e5/f5) which Black's knights and bishops seeking central posts have to avoid.

The game Leonhardt against Amos Burn in 1911, shows the effect of a mighty pawn centre. It began 1 e4 e5 2 ♘f3 ♘c6 3 ♗c4 ♗c5 4 c3 d6 5 d4 ed 6 cd ♗b6 7 ♘c3 ♘f6 8 0–0 0–0. Now

183

W.H.C.

Black threatens the common combination 9 . . . ♘xe4 10 ♘xe4 d5 which regains his piece and gets rid of the pawn centre in the process. White avoids this with **9 ♗b3** and play continued **9 . . . ♗g4 10 ♗e3 h6**. This is passive; Black would do better to keep White's centre under fire with 10 . . . ♖e8 11 ♕d3 ♗h5 and bringing his bishop to g6. The game proceeded **11 ♕d3 ♖e8 12 ♘d2 ♕e7 13 ♖ae1 ♖ad8 14 a3**. With Black's pieces so boxed in, White can leisurely cover and deprive Black of every useful looking square. **14 . . . ♕f8 15 f4** White threatens to hem in the black bishop at g4 by f5 followed by h3. Black played **15 . . . ♗c8** and White's game assumed crushing dimensions after **16 h3 ♔h8 17 g4**. (diag 184) Black tried to break out of the stranglehold by **17 . . . ♘e7 18 ♔h1 d5** but after **19 e5** had a pitiful number of squares available. The game continued **19 . . . ♘h7 20 f5 f6 21 e6 c6 22 ♗f4 ♘g8**. To have a square for the queen **23 ♘a4** White threatens 24 ♘xb6 and then to win bishop for rook by 25 ♗c7; there's a battle for some moves over this. **23 . . . ♗a5 24 ♗c2 ♕e7 25 ♕g3 b5 26 ♘c5** Black never escaped from White's grip and was forced to resign 16 moves later.

The battle of differing pawn formations is exemplified by this basic position (diag 185). White, with the d + e pawns, has a potentially cramping pawn centre; this could also advance and drive a wedge into the black position. Middle game prospects often favour White; but the position of the pieces is a vital factor; if Black survives the middle-game he may be able to create a passed pawn on the ♛-side by advancing the pawns to b4 and c3. Passed pawns increase in value as does their distance from the opposing king.

184
B

185

In the position from a grandmaster game between Gligoric (Yugoslavia) and Szabo (Hungary) (diag 186), White's three pawns to one on the queen's wing look very imposing. Play went 11 . . . a5 12 ℤb1 ab 13 ab ♘c6. Now White could be tempted by 14 b5 but then comes 14 . . . ♘e5 threatening mate (. . . ♘f3) and after 15 f4 ♘f3+ 16 ♔f2, Black can afford to give up the knight by 16 . . . ♗xc5+ 17 ♔xf3 as he obtains a great attack with 17 . . . d4 opening the diagonal b7–h1. The game continued 14 ♗g2 ℤb8 15 ♗a3 ♗d7 16 0–0 ♘a7. The squares in front of the White pawns will become havens and posts for the black pieces. 17 ℤe1 ♘e8 18 ♗c1 ♗f6 19 ♗f4 e5—first step forward of Black's pawn centre— 20 ♗d2 d4 21 ♘d5 ♗c6 22 ♘xf6+ ♛xf6 23 ♗xc6 ♛xc6 24 f4 f6 25 ♛b3+ ♔h8 26 ℤf1 ♘c7 White's pawns are firmly held, while Black's pawns are restricting White's knight and bishop. 27 ♛c4 ♘ab5 28 ℤbe1 h6 29 g4 ℤbe8 30 f5 Exchanging pawns by 30 fe fe would have given White more counterplay. 30 . . . ♛d5 31 ♛c1 ♔h7 32 ♘g3 e4 These black pawns now dominate the board. 33 ♗f4 e3 34 ♛d1 ♛c4 35 h4 ♘d5 36 g5 d3 37 ♛g4 ℤg8 This rules out any tactical resources along the g-file. 38 ♘h5 ℤe4 39 g6+ ♔h8 Now White played 40 ♛g3 but conceded the game; he has no good answer to 40 . . . d2. The centre pawns have triumphed.

Pawn centres are not always advantageous features. They can

become a target, and tie down valuable pieces to defending them. Grandmaster and author, Yuri Averbakh, set about destroying the effectiveness of White's pawn centre (diag 187) by the pawn attack **14 . . . f5**, trying to knock out the middle pawn. If White pushes on (15 e5), then the square d5 becomes available for Black's pieces—bishop, queen and perhaps knight—and Black can also build up pressure on the backward white pawn at d4. The game continued **15 ♖xc8 ♛xc8 16 ♛d2 fe 17 ♗xe4 ♘c4 18 ♗d5+ ♗e6 19 ♗xc4 ♛xc4** when White's pawn centre is broken and weak.

Pawn Endings

Even reasonably good players miscalculate pawn endings, so one is likely to gain points with even rudimentary knowledge. Diagram 188 gives an ideal position for White. His king stands here ready to shepherd the pawn over the last three fences (f6, f7, f8); Black cannot stop the pawn from queening.

The next diagram (189) is important and critical; what happens depends on whose turn it is to move. If it is White to move he can either play **1 ♔f6** leaving the black king stalemated, or write off the pawn. But when it's Black's turn to move he must vacate the queening square, **1 . . . ♔g7**, allowing White's king to occupy the shepherding position, **2 ♔e7**, and then queen.

The next position (diag 190) is an ideal one to be aimed for by the side with the pawn. If the king can reach the sixth rank in front of its pawn (unless the pawn is on an edge file, i.e. an a- or h-pawn), it's a win irrespective of who has the move. When Black moves, for

example 1 . . . ♚g8, the white king takes the shepherding position
2 ♔e7. With White to move, it's a little more complicated, 1 ♔e6
♚e8 2 f6 ♚f8 3 f7, but Black must relinquish his grip on the
shepherding square, 3 . . . ♚g7 4 ♔e7, and White queens.

The move doesn't matter in the next position (diag 191) but
accuracy is called for. By 1 . . . ♚e8 Black would lose after 2 ♔e6
♚f8 3 f7 ♚g7 4 ♔e7 and queens. Instead, Black must step straight
back by 1 . . . ♚f8 so that, after 2 ♔e6, he can go 2 . . . ♚e8 directly
confronting the white king; then White's attempts to push the pawn
home by 3 f7+ ♚f8 leads to the loss of the pawn if stalemate by
4 ♔f6 is to be avoided. Remember, king straight back . . . ♚f8, and
aim for stalemate.

Again, in diagram 192 the move counts. With it being his turn to
move, White is not assured of more than a draw; for example 1 ♔e5
♚e7—confronting directly—2 f5 ♚f7 3 f6 and, as we remember,
king straight back by 3 . . . ♚f8 leads to a draw. With the move Black
has to give ground, e.g. 1 . . . ♚e7 2 ♔g6 when White reaches the
always winning position with king on the sixth and in front of the
pawn.

These five pawn endings should be memorised. Again: from
diagram 193, king in shepherding position—a win; from diagram 194,
watch for stalemate; king on the sixth on front of the pawn—always
a win, that's the lesson of diagram 195; and in diagram 196 king
straight back, king up, king confronts (1 . . . ♚f8 2 ♔e6 ♚e8) . . .
and draws; another confrontation in diagram 197—if Black must
give way he loses.

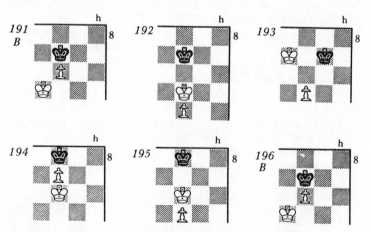

The exception to these pawn endings are also important. If the
defending king can get in front of an a-pawn or h-pawn, the game
should always be drawn, due to the increased chances of stalemate.

An important type of pawn ending is shown in diagram 198. White has two pawns to one on the queen's wing and Black three to two on the king's wing. The side that can create a passed pawn and at the same time eliminate all the opposition's pawns on that one wing generally wins. White can play **1 b5+** and bring about such a situation. At the opportune moment, White will desert his queen side pawn and proceed to mop up Black's pawns on the king's side.

Pawn Weaknesses

There are a great variety of pawn weaknesses and pawn formations that strongly influence the piece play. From diagram 199, White can give up his fianchettoed bishop at g2—something that is not lightly done—in order to exchange off the knight by **1 ♗xc6 bc** and weaken Black's pawns. The a7 pawn is isolated from the other pawns; there's no pawn on an adjacent file. The pair at c6 and c5 are doubled and isolated. When this position occurred in a 1954 Russian game, play went **2 ♕a4 ♕d7 3 ♘f3 f6 4 ♗e3 e5 5 ♘e4 ♘e6 6 ♖c1 ♖b8 7 ♕c2 ♗e7?! 8 ♘xc5 ♘xc5 9 ♗xc5 ♗xc5 10 ♕xc5 ♖xb2** when Black was suddenly faced with severe problems after the combination **11 ♘xe5** trying to fork Black's king and rook. White eventually won.

Here are three more basic pawn formations around which are woven many chess battles. In diagram 200, the important feature is

Black's isolated central pawn at d5; d5 is also the case in diagram 201; the isolated pawn can be a target, the square in front (d4) a post for an opponent's piece; in favour of it can be greater control its master exercises on the other surrounding squares. The c5+d5 pawns in diagram 202 are described as hanging pawns—there are circumstances where they are strong, and others where they are weak.

201

202

Bad Bishop

Black's bishop is badly restricted because his own pawns are fixed on dark squares in diagram 203. There's nothing in White's position that the bishop can bear on, whereas White's knight, on the other hand, can operate from either black or white squares. If White can bring his king to c5 then the black pawns begin to fall. White can try to win this ending because Black's bishop is 'bad'. In an attempt to bring his king to the desired position (c5), White starts with 1 ♔b4 and is held up after 1 . . . ♔b6; but 2 ♘a4+ throws Black more on the defensive, 2 . . . ♔c6, and the white king marginally penetrates Black's territory by 3 ♔a5. From now on White plans to drive the black king back, square by square, and edge his own king to c5. A knight check is required and happens after the manoeuvre 4 ♘c3, 5 ♘a2 and 6 ♘b4+. Black can only mark time. The knight check will lead to White following up with king to b5 and to b6 while the black king retreats to d6. Then the white knight is brought via a2 and c3 to b5 to check once more. This will force the black king out of the d6 square and thus enables the white king to come to c5. Then, after another knight move (c7 or c3) the black d-pawn will fall; White can repeat the approach to Black's remaining pawn.

A simpler, but more improbable, example of a bad bishop is seen in this made up position in diagram 204. The black pieces remain entangled through White's ability to exploit a mating possibility after 1 ♔h6 ♔h8 with 2 ♘h4; the hoped-for emergence of the bishop

into freedom 2 . . . ♗g8 would permit the knight mate at g6. Therefore Black must allow White to improve the positioning of his knight
2 . . . ♔g8 3 ♘f3 ♔h8 4 ♘e5 ♔g8 5 ♘c6 ♔h8 to 6 ♘e7; then Black,
safe as the position stands, has to move and give ground and that
means to give up his bishop. For this type of position chessplayers
have a special expression—zugzwang—literally meaning move-bound.

Extending the Bishop
After these opening moves: 1 d4 ♘f6 2 c4 g6 3 ♘c3 d5 4 ♗f4 ♗g7
5 e3 0–0 6 ♘f3 Black, among other things, will not be completely
satisfied with the scope of his bishop at g7, and may choose to play
6 . . . c5, as after 7 dc the bishop's diagonal is extended and he can
bring the queen into co-operative action by 7 . . . ♕a5. Now 8 cd
would be near suicidal because of the line opener 8 . . . ♘xd5—if
9 ♕xd5 ♗xc3+ 10 bc (not best) 10 . . . ♕xc3+ when White's rook
at a1 goes.

Extending the Rooks
I would like to switch from the use of the bishop to the extension of
the rook's development. We seem to have left them sitting at the end
of open files waiting for a chance to infiltrate the opponent's territory. In diagram 205, where do you want the white rooks to be? At
e7, to get at Black's pawns. The entry is brought about by 1 ♗e7
forcing the swap 1 . . . ♗xe7 2 ♖xe7, (b7 pawn is attacked). After
2 . . . ♖ab8 White can double along the seventh with 3 ♖d7 and
except at a cost of several pawns, Black cannot stop White following
up by the other rook to the seventh, (4 ♖1e7), when black pawns
will fall anyway.

More preparation is involved for the white rooks to break into
Black's position in diagram 206. Réti, a great Czech player, who was
White, improves everything, ready for the moment of opening up,
starting with 1 ♘c3, and this classic game continued 1 . . . ♖h8
2 ♖h3 ♖bg8 3 ♖bh1 ♕d8 4 ♘d5. Now White wants to play ♔f1

for safety reasons, then follow up with hg hg; ♔h2 ♖xh3; ♔xh3 ♖h8; ♔xh8+ ♔xh8; ♖xh8 ♔xh8 and win the f6 pawn. The game continued 4 ... gh 5 ♖xh4 ♔f7 6 ♔f2 ♔f8 7 ♖xh6 ♖xh6 8 ♖xh6 ♔g7 when the switch to the alternative way in by 9 ♕a5 left Black no suitable reply.

The position in diagram 207 is taken from a world championship game in 1948. Vasily Smyslov—to be world champion in 1957—was White and another equally famous player, Paul Keres, had Black. White would ask himself where his rooks are going to find their needed open file. The half-open c-file offers no immediate targets. Where can pawns be exchanged? At e4, b5 and maybe, but surely unlikely, at a6. Where will it be least helpful to the opponent? Black already has a rook waiting at e8 for the opening of the e-file. Where can the timing be in White's hands? Smyslov played 1 ♖ab1! He's planning b2–b4–b5. Play continued 1 ... ♘g6 2 b4 ♗d6 (if 2 ... a6 White can re-inforce his wedge with 3 a4, or if Black blocks with 2 ... b5 perhaps Black's c6-pawn will become a target for White's pieces). The pawn went on 3 b5 ♗d7 4 bc; White had a prolonged initiative and won.

Improving the Knight

After 17 moves, Nimzowitsch–Rubinstein, Dresden 1926, reached the position in diagram 208. Nimzowitsch, not happy with the scope of his knight at g3, looked round for a better square for it. g5 looked good, but how does one bring it there. Nimzowitsch played 18 ♘h1!! He could only be contemplating the journey h1–f2–h3–g5. The game went 18 ... ♗d7 19 ♘f2 ♖ae8 20 ♖fe1 ♖xe2 21 ♖xe2 ♘d8 If 21 ... ♖e8 22 ♕d5! ♘e7 23 ♕f7! wins. 22 ♘h3 ♗c6 Now 22 ... ♖e8 is met by 23 ♕h5 ♖xe2 24 ♘g5! h6 25 ♕g6! forcing mate at h7 or h5. 23 ♕h5 g6 24 ♕h4 ♔g7 25 ♕f2! ♗c5 26 b4 ♗b6 27 ♕h4! ♖e8 28 ♖e5! ♘f7 29 ♗xf7 ♕xf7 30 ♘g5 At last 30 ... ♕g8 31 ♖xe8 ♗xe8 32 ♕e1! This is a splendid example of play for control of the e-file. 32 ... ♗c6 33 ♕e7+ ♔h8

34 b5!! If now 34 . . . ab 35 ♘e6 h5 36 ♕f6+ ♔h7 37 ♘g5+ ♔h6 38 ♗b4! introduces the bishop with decisive effect. **34 . . . ♕g7 35 ♕xg7 ♔xg7 36 bc** and won in some moves.

Improving the King

All White's pieces in the position from the Kostić-Capablanca match in 1919 (diag 209) are tied up by the pins f6—f1 and h2—d2. Capablanca examines the position to find how he can improve his pieces and add to the pressure on Kostić's position. His king is not doing much. If it could be brought all the way to the square b3 then Black could exchange all the pieces off at f2 and help himself to White's queen's side pawn. Capablanca played **51 . . . ♚e7!** and he plans then to protect his rook at h2 by . . . ♗g3 and after that to proceed with the king's journey. Therefore Kostich tried **52 b4** but after **52 . . . c4xb3 53 ♘d3 ♖xd2** he resigned as after 54 ♖xf6 Black has the desperado 54 . . . ♖xd3+! emerging with a bishop up.

Bishops of Opposite Colours

The presence of bishops of opposite colours on the board has a distinctive influence. In diagram 210 the ending is drawn as White's bishop is useless for disputing f7 with Black's bishop. In endings bishops of opposite colour are a well-known drawing factor. However, in complex middle game positions, the fact that the bishops are operating on different colour diagonals tends to limit the exchanging off of supporting major pieces (queens and rooks); in such circumstances the bishop on opposite colours can add force to an attack.

Exchanges

Do not shirk the solution of exchanging off an opponent's well placed piece, even queens. It is a common misconception that the game is less interesting with queens off; it is often harder.

Shifting the Emphasis

Wing attacks are best countered by solid distractions in the centre. In his game with Vajda in the match Moscow–Budapest 1949, faced with White's king side pawn storm, (diag 211), the Russian grandmaster, Kotov, successfully shifted the battle arena to the centre by **1 . . . b4! 2 ♘e2 e5! 3 f5** if 3 g5 ♘g4 4 ♗xg4 ♗xg4 5 f5 d5! **3 . . . d5!** Therefore before one embarks on an all-out flank attack one takes steps to have a solid or firm centre.

210

211
B

5 Human factors

Perfect Games are Drawn

The main battle of the chessboard is within yourself! You lose because you make mistakes or you fail to adjust yourself to changes in the nature of the position or the conditions. And you'll do your utmost to prove that some factor external to your brain was responsible for the failure. It is a basic assumption that a chess game cannot be lost without the making of a traceable error.

A perfectly played game should end in a draw. Somewhere between the playing of moves by White and Black, usually after Black's, a state of balance exists. From this players develop a sense of balance that provides the 'feel' of the position. The tilting of this balance will help one to decide whether to play to win or to draw or to complicate or on what other decision arises.

A well-fought draw may be artistically satisfying. That for instance would apply to the game Geller–Golombek played in the big Budapest tournament in 1952; it went **1 d4 ♘f6 2 c4 e6 3 ♘c3 ♗b4 4 e3 c5 5 a3 cd 6 ab dc 7 ♘f3!? cb 8 ♗xb2 d5 9 c5 b6?!** 9 ... 0–0 is safer. 10 ♗b5+, possibly better is 10 ♗d3. **10 ... ♗d7 11 ♗xd7+ ♘fxd7! 12 ♕c2! ♘c6! 13 ♗xg7 ♘xb4! 14 ♕b1 ♖g8 15 c6! ♘xc6 16 ♕xh7 ♘f6!!** diag 212 **17 ♗xf6 ♕xf6 18 ♕xg8+ ♔d7 19 ♘e5+! ♘xe5!** If 19 ... ♕xe5 20 ♕xf7+ wins. **20 ♕xa8 ♘f3+ 21 gf.** On 21 ♔e2 ♕b2+ 22 ♔xf3 ♕f6+ perpetually checks. **21 ... ♕xa1+ 22 ♔e2 ♕b2+** Draw agreed. It's also perpetual check after 23 ♔f1 ♕b1+ 24 ♔g2 ♕g6+ 25 ♔h3 ♕h5+.

Need for Creative Ideas

But success in chess is measured by the scoring of wins. And that requires imperfections and the intrusion of human factors.

Where two players are well-matched in knowledge, technique and temperament, success still may go to the one who is able to conjure forth time-consuming problems at critical junctures and in general to create sound new positional and attacking ideas. And that is what top class chess is about.

Over the years the pieces and the board remain the same; there are certain areas of knowledge, particularly in the endings, which are accepted as fact; certain moves in the openings lead to palpably lost positions or mate—these are known and avoided. But there are very large 'grey' areas where certainties do not exist and in which the great players, whose characteristics are so different, can impose, change and refute ideas and approaches. In other words there is a constant flux within chess that keeps it very much alive. For example the openings of today may be has-beens tomorrow.

PROCEDURE FOR THINKING

Probing the Position

What is he trying to do? This is the number one question in chess-playing. You have to ask yourself this, every time your opponent moves. There are varying shades of this question which could, for instance, depend on whether you are attacking or defending. The great players, even when they move in a flash, will still have asked themselves this question.

Every move adds to the pressure on some square(s) and subtracts from the pressure against others. Look every time, even if only for a fraction of a second, at each fresh square attacked by the piece the opponent's hand has just quitted. By feeding your brain with this information and by asking a series of questions, you develop a sense of the balances and imbalances within a position.

Let's look at an interesting game and examine some of the thinking processes behind the moves. After 1 e2–e4 e7–e5 2 ♘g1–f3 ♘b8–c6 3 ♗f1–c4, this bishop move adds pressure to the squares b3/d5/e6/f7/f1; it also weakens the hold on g2/h3 and c4. N.B. A piece occupying a square does not control it.

In return for information the brain's thinking centres may provide an almost instant reply. And more than 50 per cent of the time this will be the move you will finally end up by playing. But—a very big but—it rarely pays to accept the first reaction and make a quick move on the board. You are not playing good chess if one move in every three is a bad one. There are further questions and probing to which the first reaction should be exposed. In this, human qualities like courage, recklessness, resolution, timidity, will play an important role.

I want to concentrate on the steps required to develop depth in both reflective thinking and actual calculation. You should learn, when looking at each square newly controlled—either before your own or after his move—to visualise the piece as going to that square and to scan (in your mind) the further squares that could be controlled. One's brain quickly learns to reject the ridiculous and improbable in a matter of hundredths of a second. The second and natural extension deeper is to trace paths for each of one's chess-

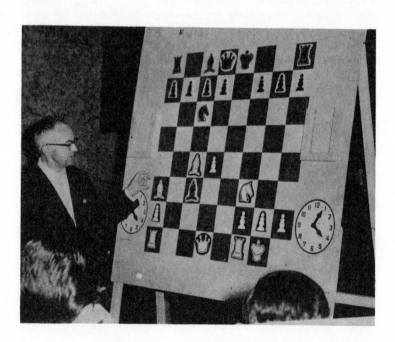

men and to visualise and create ideal lines of action and posts for them. You would be advised to do this for your opponent's pieces as well.

To continue our game 3 . . . ♗f8–c5 4 c2–c3 ♘g8–f6 5 d2–d4 e5xd4 6 c3xd4 ♗c5–b4+ 7 ♘b1–c3 ♘f6xe4. . . . In trying to reach a decision on what to play here, White may take into account that the ideal positioning for his rook at h1 would be at e1 with pressure directed along the e-file towards the black king. . . . 8 0–0 White threatens ♘c3xe4.

You feed as much relevant data as possible into your thinking centres and hope they will connect up various features of the position and help you to make plans.

The game–8 . . . ♘e4xc3–bishop takes, is more usual–9 b2xc3 ♗b4xc3? It should be too risky for Black to go picking up pawns and leaving his main forces at home. A strong player would choose 9 . . . d7-d5 instead. It being his move the white player should ask the following questions.

The Questions
First question: What is Black trying to do? Answer: He would like to take my rook in the corner.

Second question: How does Black's capture affect my plan? Answer: I can't play ♖e1+ yet–the bishop at c3 covers e1. There's nothing in ♕e2+–Black can interpose his queen. Can I bring more pieces into action, as I had hoped when making the castling move? ♖b1–the rook would be on an open file, but it doesn't seem to be attacking or moving to anywhere important. White has sacrificed two pawns for attacking hopes.

Third question: What to do? Direction needed and a decision wanted. Do we have to save the rook on a1? Can we get Black's bishop off the diagonal a5–e1? Black's bishop at c3 is loose (i.e. not protected). Can advantage be taken of that? White can play 10 ♗xf7+ ♚xf7 11 ♕b3+; White would regain one of the sacrificed pawns and make Black's king something of a target. It's worth playing.

Fourth question: Have I a better move? When you learn to ask yourself this question, you have an essential ingredient for becoming a good player. Better moves are missed all the time because this question is not asked often enough. In order to try to stop himself from moving too quickly, the great German player, Dr. Siegbert Tarrasch, used to sit on his hands. Have I a better move? Take another look at the whole position on the chessboard. Does it matter if Black takes the rook? He would be putting his bishop out of play. Then I could play ♖e1+. Black could answer the check with . . . ♚e8–f8 or . . . ♘c6–e7. What could I usefully do in the meantime?

If the brain connects the two squares (e7 and f8), which Black could use in order to defend himself against White's ♖e1+, I might find the move ♗c1—a3. Then if Black continues . . . ♗xa1 White would win Black's queen by 11 ♖e1+ ♘e7 12 ♗xe7—when this line is calculated completely out we'll find that material will be approximately equal, but that White's pieces are more active.

Fifth question: Is the intended move safe? Am I being stupid? This question is designed to make one take a last look at the position before moving, but it must be accompanied by a change in perspective. The mind can tackle very involved problems and, at the same time, completely overlook something simple. The number of blunders and oversights can be radically reduced through asking this question. Having made up your mind what to play, you shut off all the work that you've done on the position and then, you eye the position again in a different light.

Continuing the Game

White played **10 ♗c1—a3!** If 10 . . . ♗c3xa1 11 ♖f1—e1+ ♘c6—e7 12 ♗a3xe7 ♕d8xe7 13 ♖e1xe7+ ♔e8xe7 14 ♕d1xa1. The position, for the moment, is stabilised. How do we assess this position? A material count would show: White: queen—9–10 points, bishop and knight each just over 3 points—say 16 points for the pieces and 5 for the pawns—total 21; Black: 2 rooks—10 points, bishop 3+, 7 for the pawns—total 20 and a bit points. There is not much between the two sides. White's slight edge is certainly not enough to ensure him of a win. But an 'activity count' shows a definite plus for the white pieces; the two factors combine—very slight material plus together with superior mobility means that White has a clear advantage—not clearly a win but everything to play for.

The game continued **10 . . . d7—d6**. The main alternative is 10 . . . d7—d5. **11 ♖a1—c1** (after asking the questions) **11 . . . ♗c3—a5** (diag 213). It looks as if Black wants to castle, bring his other pieces into play and remain two pawns up. Where can White attack? Black's

213
W

bishop on a5 still stops ♖e1+. This bishop is protected by the knight at c6. White can drive the knight away by 12 d5 (say 12 . . . ♘e7) and then fork Black's king and bishop by 13 ♕a4+; but Black defends both threats with 13 . . . c6, enabling the queen to protect the bishop. Can White improve on this? Can he play a similar attack using a different order of moves? White played **12 ♕d1—a4** White threatens 13 d5 to take advantage of the pin on the diagonal a4—e8, as well as trying to drive away the bishop's protector. Black rejected the moves . . . 0—0 and . . . ♗d7 and replied **12 . . . a7—a6.** He wants to play . . . b5 forking White's queen and bishop. White decided that Black would gain sufficient counterplay after 13 d5 b5 and looked for a better move. He played **13 ♗c4—d5.** This threatens to take Black's knight with check, thus winning the bishop; 13 . . . b5 would be met by 14 ♗xc6+ winning two pieces.

Black played **13 . . . ♗a5—b6.** White can now consider ♖e1+. But there are also interesting complications if he should capture on c6, e.g. 14 ♗xc6+ bxc6 15 ♕xc6+ at the same time attacking a black rook; but Black can defend himself with 15 . . . ♗d7 and the rook is protected. Pity that White does not still have this bishop at d5 as then he could afford to take the rook. How about if he had initially taken on c6 with the rook instead of the bishop? The game could go 14 . . . bxc6 15 ♕xc6+ ♗d7 16 ♕xa8. White played **12 ♖c1xc6** and Black answered **14 . . . ♗c8—d7.** White hadn't expected that. He hadn't given the last look round the position before taking the knight! The rook is pinned and cannot retreat.

Trouble

White is in trouble. Black will be able to recapture on c6 at his leisure and White will have lost the equivalent of two more pawns. What to do?

When something unexpected happens on the chessboard, you should allow yourself time to recover from the shock condition. There are varying degrees of shock; most players are susceptible; it is not easily diagnosed; but first reactions are suspect. When surprised, you mustn't immediately react with a counter move. Don't try to convince the opponent that you were waiting for his move! Just allow time for the body and mind to re-adjust; let there be time for the normal chemical constituents of the blood stream to be restored. Many terrible blunders are made under shocked circumstances, moves which are incomprehensible when looked at afterwards. Examine the position calmly.

White can stop Black from castling. Is there better? What can be got for the rook? If 15 ♖xd6 ♗xa4 White has 16 ♖xd8+ but after 16 . . . ♔xd8 seems to the equivalent of three pawns down without concrete attacking prospects. That would be almost hopeless. But

White, determined not to lose, rechecks his calculations. After
15 ♖xd6 . . . 15 . . . ♗xa4 . . . White can sandwich in the check
16 ♖e1+. Black goes 16 . . . ♔f8 and then 17 ♖xd8 is in check—no,
even better, it is checkmate because it is double check. Now take it
coolly. Players often blunder when they are excited. Once more
15 ♖xd6 ♗xa4 16 ♖e1+—Black has an alternative. He can play
16 . . . ♕e7. Analysing further, we reach after 17 ♖xe7 ♔xe7 18
♖xb6+ a position where White will have won a bishop and knight
for a rook—material advantage.

Finishing the Game

After further analysis and rechecking, White played 15 ♖c6xd6 and
the game continued 15 . . . c7xd6 16 ♖f1—e1+ ♔e8—f8 17 ♗a3xd6+
♔f8—g8. The king has no flight square. 18 ♘f3—g5! g7—g6! 18 . . .
♕xg5 19 ♕xd7 threatens many mates. 19 ♘g5xf7 ♕d8—c8 20
♘f7—d8+ ♔g8—g7 21 ♖e1—e7+ ♔g7—f6 22 ♖e7—f7+ ♔f6—g5
23 ♗d6—f4+ ♔g5—h5 24 ♖f7—d7 White is ahead materially while
the black king is in a mating net. The game was wound up by 24 . . .
♗b6xd8 25 ♕a4—d1+ ♔h5—h4 26 g2—g3+ ♔h4—h3 27 ♗d5—g2
checkmate.

The Five Questions

The lesson of this section is about the five questions that need to be
asked before making each move. They are:

  1 What's he/she trying to do?
  2 How does it affect my plan?
  3 What to do?
  4 Have I better?
  5 Have I the position in perspective?

Some of the procedures and questions asked can be acquired by
experience, but training in these methods can mean that your use of
them is more economical and effective; they could also provide a
basis for increasing one's capacity for thinking. Further, a logical
chess training can prevent the development of sloppy thinking
methods such as permanently handicap many players.

General Advice

Learn the questions, and improve the form of the questions, that
provide information for your thinking centres.

Play through good grandmaster games, that are annotated in
reasonable depth, in order to acquire ideas and have models for
cohesive chains of thought.

MISTAKES AND BLUNDERS

How and why are mistakes made? A coolly detached diagnosis in this direction plus the determined application of corrections can make a tremendous advance in one's results possible. Great players make many minor errors of judgement but their tremendous will, and perhaps further factors, makes them nearly free of gross blunders.

The reasons for errors and blunders include the following:

Errors are made through *moving too quickly*, for a variety of reasons; when using clocks in serious tournament and match play this may come about through shortage of time.

Errors and gross blunders come about through *fatigue* and *poor physical condition*. An example of fatigue occurred in the 1974 open tournament at Las Palmas (diag 214). Black, in a winning position, played without calculation 1 . . . c5xd4?? completely oblivious to the freedom suddenly acquired by White's c-pawn and that it could queen first; he actually sat back in his chair looking very contented.

In the Las Palmas game, fatigue was the main issue, but there was another factor. Krogius, the Russians' specialist chess psychologist, writes that, in appraising a position, there is a tendency and danger to transfer part of a past or passing position to a new situation. Black, having accepted the immovable feature of White's c-pawn for most of the game, in his mind carried that impression on to the position that would result after 1 . . . cd.

As an example of this *retained image* Krogius cites the game Ilyin-Zhenevsky v. Nenarokov (diag 215). Note that the black king's position at e8 and where it might seek sanctuary. Ilyin-Zhenevsky calculated the variation 1 ♗f7+ ♔f8 2 ♕h6+ ♔xf7 3 ♖f6+ ♔e8 4 ♕f8+ ♔d7 5 ♕g7+ ♔ back 6 ♖f8 mating—a neat finish. But what happened? The game went 1 ♗f7+ ♔f8 2 ♕h6+ ♔xf7 3 ♖f6+ and Black played 3 . . . ♔g8! and gained the advantage. Why—wrote Ilyin-Zhenevsky—should I have overlooked such an obvious move as

214
B

215
W

3 . . . ♔g8? The answer is in the position diagrammed. White strongly covers the g8 square with his queen and bishop; it's a most improbable haven for the black king; it was not considered.

Generally players tend to *look at sectors* or parts of the board and very rarely at the board or position as a whole. This can lead to oversights. Before making a move it is a useful habit to make a sweep of the entire board.

Relaxation is the cause of many blunders, and there are many ways in which relaxation comes about, such as sagging from tiredness, taking refreshment, outside distractions and conversations. A typical form, when winning, is to bask in the admiring glances of friends or consterned looks of rivals, or to start to count one's chickens before they are hatched by thinking about the effects of winning on one's rating or prospects. If one relaxes, don't move quickly; wait for some tension and purposefulness to creep back into one's frame.

Changes in the position, like suddenly becoming aware that one is winning, can lead to *nervousness* and want of confidence. Time may be needed in order to re-adjust one-self. The further problem, rigidity of outlook, can lead to the missing of many opportunities.

When something suddenly goes wrong through any of the listed circumstances one can become shocked. *Shock* is a common problem that is not readily diagnosed. Yet if you move quickly in that condition you can make the most incredible blunders. If something unpleasant happens unexpectedly, suspect shock and warped thinking and take your time—some minutes—to recover. Diagram 216 is from a world championship qualifying tournament in 1964. The Hungarian grandmaster, Lengyel, played the bad 41 . . . ♖6xe2+. His opponent (Darga of West Berlin) must have had sudden visions that after 42 ♖xe2 ♗xh4+ his king would have to go to g2 and he would lose a rook; therefore he immediately resigned! When shown that he had 43 ♔e3 with winning chances, all he could do was clap his hands to his head. Both players must have retained the image

216
B

that e3 was not available to White's king because of the effect from the black rook at e6.

An exciting game is rarely blunder free. Excitement can lead to lack of caution. While you are winning against a stronger or more famous player is the time for utter calm—it's better to enjoy the win afterwards.

Time Pressure

Many games are decided by mistakes in time-trouble. It is quite common for players to leave themselves very little time within which to make many moves. This will require high speed thinking and decision taking from them. Experts can move at a rate of about one move per second and maintain a fairly high standard of play, but this requires an even rhythm of play by the opponent and little tension within the position.

Tendencies of those in time pressure include:

1 the adoption of forcing lines,
2 simplifying,
3 choosing tactical solutions and abandoning long range planning,
4 adoption of non-committal and relatively passive continuations, and
5 over-rating merits of opponent's active opportunities.

In addition to shock and other error factors, some players in serious time pressure become hypnotised by the movement of the clock or spend much of their time nervously glancing at it.

If you are in time trouble and you are stuck for a plan, Len Barden recommends you improve your worst placed piece.

Nikolai Krogius, Spassky's psychological second, wrote that there is no place for great startling discoveries while in extreme time pressure—the important thing is to succeed in making moves that are not bad.

To speed up one's own moves against an opponent in time trouble would be ill-advised; it's better to work out multi-move plans or even to forget about the time-trouble and play to one's own schedule.

Can one be cured of the fault of being habitually in time-trouble? Some people enjoy the excitement and it is doubtful if any treatment will help.

A serious method is to set yourself subsidiary time controls, say 10 moves in 25 minutes, 16 in 65 minutes, 24 in 105, 32 in 135 minutes and 40 in 2½ hours, or even more seriously play special training games in which you have to adhere to the subsidiary time controls at all costs, the quality of play being a secondary consideration. Somehow you must get into yourself that unpleasant decisions

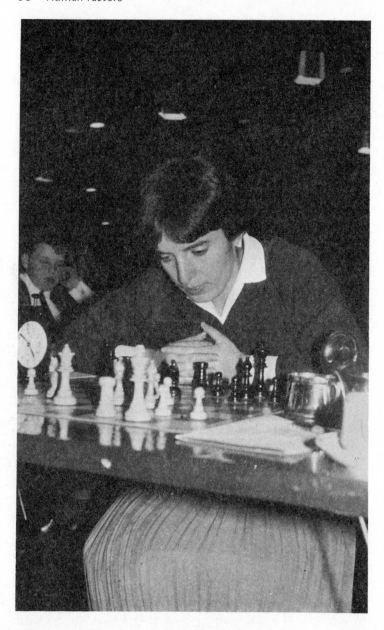

must be made without taking long, without seeking much of improbabilities and without striving for absolute perfection.

There are other approaches to trying to curb undisciplined

handling of the allocated time. Great players go through an impressive amount of work in a limited time. Of course their experienced first glance will eliminate most of the implausible possibilities. But this means that they can direct a very intensive search of the valid possibilities. Then they try to check the calculation of a variation only once and avoid a common sloppy habit of going over and over an endless treadmill of a variation hoping that something will turn up. I recommend checking calculations no more than twice.

One way of increasing one's work ratio is to play clock games with fast time limits such as five minutes each! It is important when playing such quick games to take them very seriously and to use them for testing ideas and if one is getting into a slap-happy or punch-drunk state to bring a session of such play to a rapid halt.

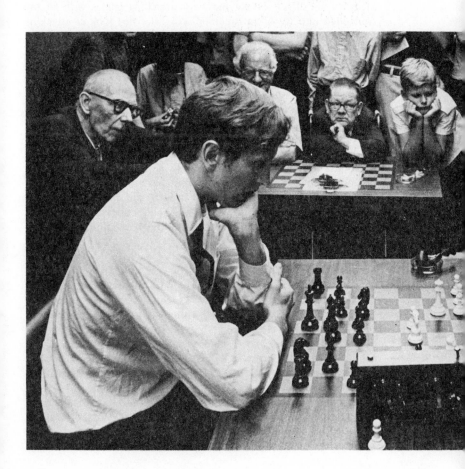

Endings

Many players wilfully neglect the endings, completely oblivious to the extra confidence that one can play with if one is prepared to play into and not avoid endings. Endings are principally about the promotion of pawns. The general rule applicable to other stages of the game—use your pieces actively—can in the endings be supplemented by the important one of using your king aggressively. Rooks are placed behind both your own advancing pawns on the way to queening and your opponent's similarly advancing passed pawns.

If you are pawns up, tend to exchange the back row pieces and not pawns. Advance passed pawns as quickly as reasonably possible, covering umbrella permitting!

Self-Assessment

Many of us dream of playing fiery attacking games with all the controlled ferocity of an Alekhine or a Tal. They look at attacking moves when they first look at the position. They have an instant awareness of the tactical possibilities. How can one get at the throat of the opponent's position? The great attacking player must in addition have a creative flair for new twists in the opening.

What sort of move do we produce at a time of crisis? Attacking? Non-committal? Counter-attacking? Balanced? Passive? Defensive? Positionally strengthening? What sort of move is the first one we look at? Which tendency triumphs if we look long and hard at the position? The opening we choose should depend on the answer to these questions.

Look at the position in diag 217. You have the black pieces. Your opponent has two more pawns than you and his bishop (c6) is threatening to take your rook (a8) and follow up with d4 and 0–0. What is your first reaction? What would be your considered reply? Turn to p. 155 for discussion.

Seeing Ahead

How far one can see ahead is a favourite talking point. In some positions the answer can be—none for certain. In others, especially when there is a forced variation, without branches, the answer can be a large number chess-wise. An experienced chessplayer develops islands of knowledge, each island being a particular type of position about which he has certain judgements. A sample type—'Black has a bad bishop and therefore has an inferior position.' Calculation can be limited to charting a course between such islands.

Another way to see ahead is, in one's mind, to shift the pieces to ideal squares and then to work backwards and forwards to see if the ideal can be achieved. Have a look at the position in diagram 218. The black pieces are curiously constricted. Note that after 1 . . . ♔b2 the black pieces are stalemated. White would like to win and even to give an early mate.

What mating position can be visualised? At the moment the black king is in check to the bishop. If the white rook (c6) stood instead at b3 then Black would be double checked and mated. Can such a position be constructed? The rook would have had to move from d3 and take on b3 to give the double check. What was Black's previous move to that? ♔b2–b1! How did it get to b2? White's rook somewhere else uncovered the bishop to give check—♖e4–e3+. From the final position we can work our way back. The complete solution has one extra twist in that after 1 . . . ♔b2 the stalemate is released by 2 ♖g6 allowing 2 . . . ♔b1; then White can check on alternative moves, by 3 ♖f6+ ♔b2 4 ♖f5 ♔b1 5 ♖f4+ ♔b2 6 ♖e4 ♔b1 7 ♖e3+ ♔b2 8 ♖d3 ♔b1 9 ♖xb3++ mate. White, by visualising the end position, has been enabled to see eight moves ahead.

6 Planning your openings

Opening Knowledge

The most feared aspect of modern chess is knowledge. There is a huge outpouring of specialist opening books (see p. 158 for a list of recommended books), books giving the games of important current events and periodicals. For instance, the twice-yearly Yugo-slav publication *Chess Informator* has 1400 games annually. To try to keep up to date seems an impossible labour.

One wants results to depend on ability at, and understanding of, chess. Nobody wants to lose to, or be saddled with a manifestly inferior game by, an opponent who has simply memorised a great number of grandmaster games, and particularly if you think you are superior in most other aspects. And most players can't afford to give up their job to study all the available material, though they don't want to be outside the current thinking and ideas about chess.

Only young people have a memory storage capacity sufficient to cope with the quantity of games that it may be useful to know. Older people need to try and formulate guide rules and what are called principles to help them. Neither method is completely self-sufficient.

All players, young and old, should play through some master games in their entirety. One remembers games and the associated opening better.

It is normal for players to specialise in a limited range of open-ings and to acquire a knowledge within the selected repertoire. The procedure would work out thus.

You would decide, stage 1 which opening to play as White. 2: list the systems with which your opponents are likely to reply, and 3: prepare the outline of a plan against each system. When preparing for playing as Black, you come in at stage 2 and add stage 4, the preparation of specific variations against stage 3. But first, what is one trying to do at the beginning of the game?

Opening Aims

One aims to bring the back row pieces to squares and lines where they will strongly influence the course of play. One tries at the same time to frustrate the opponent's efforts to do the same. These aims remain the same throughout the game.

If there is no specific target, take the trouble to improve the scope of each piece. Give some thought as to where they will stand best. For example: put a knight in the corner of an empty board (diag 219). The circles show the squares to which the piece can go. There are only two (f2 and g3), but if the knight is further up the board its range increases to three and four (diags 220 and 221). The circles in diagram 222 show that on g3 (or any other post on the second frame—squares g2–g7–b7–b2–g2) the knight commands six squares, and on any of the sixteen inner squares of the chessboard (f3–f6–c6–c3–f3), e.g. f3, (diag 223), there's a choice of eight squares immediately available. A knight takes time to hop from one wing to the other—from a central square it's not far to any outer square.

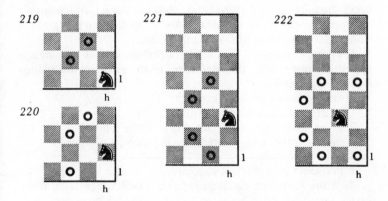

In actual play the board is cluttered with obstacles from one's own pieces and dangers from the opponent's; opposing pawns can be set to act as minefields. But generally the aim is to bring knights into, and operate them from, the central squares.

Bishops have a similar increase in scope. From the outer ring they might go to seven squares; the next ring in could add the number to nine, and so on. In the central four squares (e4/e5/d5/d4) the total could be thirteen. The rule is—operate knights and bishops towards and from the centre.

Rooks are very different. Wherever they stand on the board they can go to a maximum of fourteen squares. In fact the rooks operate best at long range. Being in the centre can be an embarrassment to them. Rooks are best stationed on open files, to await the exchange of the minor pieces—knights and bishops—before penetrating into enemy territory.

It's difficult to lay down firm rules for the queen. Lone raids are generally frowned on. She is at her best as a co-operative piece. Fixed placing is a rarity. Even early centralisation has its drawbacks—because of her high value, she can attract and help the opponent's pieces to better squares. My advice is—keep the queen in readiness to co-operate with your other pieces.

The king is normally kept safely out of the way of its own and opposition pieces until the later stages of the game. In the endings it can be vigorously used.

Pawns are moved for four reasons:

1 to free one's own pieces;
2 to be exchanged, and thus create either open files for the rooks or other ways of breaching the enemy's position;
3 to be promoted;
4 to restrict the opponent's activity.

As White starts, the initial struggle can readily be between White having one more piece active and Black, after his move, just managing to keep level. This particular aspect is noticeable most in positions where similar central pawn moves are made such as 1 e4 e5 2 ♘f3 ♘c6 3 d4. This factor is responsible for the statistics of a much greater number of wins for the white pieces.

If you have a choice between which piece to move, it is a good rule to play the one that has the least number of options. In the position after 1 e4 e5 (diag 224), the knight on g1 has one main route to the centre (via f3 to e5) while the bishop on f1 has—as our experience tells us—posts both at c4 and at b5. Therefore most people prefer to play 2 ♘g1—f3 rather than to move the bishop. This is the theorising behind the general instruction of 'knights before bishops'; of course there are plenty of exceptions to the rule.

Summarising this information, we can plan our power set-up. Knights and bishops are to function across the central squares. Rooks will need open files which may necessitate an exchange of pawns. The queen will be kept at the ready but off the back row out of the way of the rooks. The king is to be tucked safely away.

Harmonious Development

The next step, which should be self-evident, is that we should dispose our pieces and pawns in such a manner that they work in harmony together. They should not only stand well individually but should work as a team. The side that has the best in both factors must have the better chances of winning.

Let us look at a good example of harmonious development by White. 1 e4 e5 2 &c4 &f6 3 d3. This opens a way for the other bishop. 3 . . . &c5 4 &c3 d6 5 f4 White is preparing a file for his rook at h1, as after White has castled his rook will be posted actively on f1. 5 . . . &c6 6 &f3 &g4 7 &a4 This is to eliminate the black bishop on the c5–g1 diagonal; it's holding up White's castling. 7 . . . &b6 8 h3 &xf3 9 &xf3 &d4 10 &f2 (diag 225). Now White is ready to continue with such moves as &xb6, c3, 0–0, &e3 and &ae1 satisfactorily completed the first stage of the opening—his immediate mobilisation. Before him, however, stretches a long continual struggle to improve the position of his pieces until they completely dominate the board. And this is where factors like stamina, will and determination play their part.

225
B

The depth to which you prepare your repertoire must depend on two factors, the calibre of the opposition and the standard reached in one's own play.

Beginner's Plan

If you are a beginner you may be plagued by opponents who keep trying to inflict the four move checkmate (1 e4, 2 &c4, 3 &h5 and 4 &xf7) on you. You can begin to cure them by answering move 1 e2–e4 with 1 . . . e7–e6—just one square—and when they persist with 2 &f1–c4 to attack it by 2 . . . d7–d5; your d5 pawn is supported by the e-pawn and the queen. If White takes (3 e4xd5), you recapture by 3 . . . e6xd5. The white bishop's diagonal c4—f7 has been blocked off and you can keep it blocked.

When, after 1 e2—e4 e7—e6 White tries to vary the approach by playing 2 ♕d1—h5, the queen can be driven away by 2 . . . ♘g8—f6 and then next move perhaps play 3 . . . d7—d5. When White varies once more by 2 ♕d1—f3 play 2 . . . d7—d5. Indeed you can safely answer practically every method of White's by the two moves 1 . . . e7—e6 and 2 . . . d7—d5.

Simple Repertoire

Here as a sample is a very simple form of Black repertoire, with a plan to answer each important White opening. When Black, you meet:

1 e4 with 1 . . . e5
1 d4 with 1 . . . d5
1 ♘f3 with 1 . . . d5
1 c4 with 1 . . . e5

Against odd moves like 1 b3 there's 1 . . . e5 and against 1 g3, also 1 . . . e5; even if 1 f4, 1 . . . e5 is a good reply. In other words— when it's safe to play . . . e5 you do so; otherwise you fall back on . . . d5.

As White plays 1 e4. It's not a bad repertoire.

When you have decided on your repertoire, keep refreshing it by playing through the moves of relevant games published in newspaper columns or the more specialist sources. You should make a habit of playing through the entire moves of these games; that way a greater impact is made on your memory and besides you are likely to add to your general understanding.

Universal Repertoires for Black

If you have very restricted time for study you'll be tempted to base your defence on a universal system applicable against any opening that White can come up with; then one confines one's study to the formations and conditions that will force you to modify your system.

The first universal system that comes to mind is one that extends the Beginners Plan. Black plays 1 . . . e6 and 2 . . . d5 against practically every set-up that White can adopt. This may be followed by . . . c5, with the knight at g8 going to e7 or f6 and the other knight (b8) usually being developed at c6. The bishop f8 can go to e7 or d6 or c5 or b4 depending on circumstances. There may be problems with the other bishop, but these are not insoluble; it could be finachettoed by . . . b6 and . . . ♗b7. In any repertoire as Black, it is impossible to lay down the files that should be opened or fought over for the rooks—which files will depend on how White disposes his pawns. But this opening (1 . . . e6 followed by 2 . . . d5) establishes the basis for a solid, sound position.

The reversed system with the centre pawns (1 . . . d6 and 2 . . . e5) is a possibility; but White can complicate its set-up after 1 d4 d6 by playing 2 ♘f3; Black will need to prepare the . . . e5 move by . . . ♘bd7 or . . . ♘c6 or by getting rid of White's knight by 2 . . . ♗g4 and later exchanging it.

Universal with . . . c6 and . . . d5

A third universal system of defence for Black is the combination 1 . . . c6 followed by 2 . . . d5. 1 e4 c6 2 d4 d5 is the Caro-Kann Defence and 1 d4 c6 2 c4 d5 is the Slav Defence. In both defences Black keeps open the c8—h3 diagonal for developing his c8-bishop.

Modern Universal Systems

The universal system that is currently interesting the world's leading players is based on the moves . . . g6 followed by . . . ♗g7 together with . . . d6 with diagonals open for both bishops. It may not matter which Black plays first, 1 . . . g6 or 1 . . . d6. In due time the d6 pawn supports advances like c7—c5 and e7—e5, while Black's pawn formation is elastic enough to contemplate such additions as . . . c7—c6, . . . a7—a6 and . . . b7—b5 or . . . b7—b6. Even this re-arrangement . . . c7—c6 and . . . d6—d5 or the early advance . . . f7—f5 could be feasible.

These systems of defence are covered by Ray Keene and George Botterill's books *The Pirc Defence* and *The Modern Defence*, supplemented by another Batsford book *The King's Indian Defence*, written by three British champions, Ray Keene, Bill Hartston and Len Barden.

In this modern system, the knight g8 usually comes to f6, but there are a few odd lines where the knight travels via e7 or h6. One must be even less dogmatic about the development of the other black pieces, but then, the whittling away of dogma is a characteristic of our age.

King's Indian Defence

If White adopts the order 1 d4 g6 2 c4 d6 3 ♘c3 ♗g7 4 e4 Black can revert to the well-known King's Indian Defence lines with knight out 4 . . . ♘f6 (diag 226).

Against the Sämisch system (5 f3) a very up-to-date combative idea is 5 . . . ♘c6 6 ♗e3 and now, as his position is not under pressure, Black can prepare by 6 . . . a6 7 ♘ge2 ♖b8 to open a file on the queen's wing; a 1971 Russian game continued 8 ♘c1 e5 9 d5 ♘d4 White could now win a pawn by 10 ♗xd4 ed 11 ♕xd4, but

Black would obtain plenty of counterplay after 11 . . . 0–0. **10 ♘1e2 c5 11 dc en passant bc 12 ♘xd4 ed 13 ♗xd4 ♖xb2** Now, when White mistakenly tried to exploit the situation of the intruding rook by **14 ♘b5**, Black hit back hard with **14 . . . ♘xe4!** After **15 ♗xb2 ♕a5+ 16 ♘c3 ♗xc3+ 17 ♗xc3 ♕xc3+ 18 ♔e2 ♗e6**, with its further threats to the white king, brought about White's acknowledgment of defeat.

These moves worked well for Black against the Sämisch set-up (f3, ♗e3 and ♘ge2 for White), but would not necessarily do against other plans. White could play, from diagram 226, **5 ♗e2 0–0 6 ♘f3 e5**. This is an important point of divergences.

Petrosian's plan **7 d5 ♘bd7 8 ♗g5** (diag 227) is met by ♔-side manoeuvres (**8 . . . h6 9 ♗h4 g5 10 ♗g3 ♘h5**) when, as compensation for the weakening of his king's side, Black can hope to play . . . f5 and have the better placed pieces.

Yet another system for White arises from the moves **7 0–0 ♘c6 8 d5**; after **8 . . . ♘e7** Black can aim to play . . . ♘d7 (or even . . . ♘e8), followed by . . . f5.

If White sets up a massive pawn centre by **5 f4 0–0 6 ♘f3**, Black can challenge it with **6 . . . c5** (diag 228), and if **7 d5** continue to chivy it with **7 . . . e6**.

Against another popular White plan of development, **4 g3 ♘f6 5 ♗g2 0–0 6 ♘c3**, can be commended the system **6 . . . ♘c6 7 0–0 ♗f5** used by Fischer against Petrosian in 1966.

One cannot over-emphasise that, in setting up a framework of openings, you must fill in that frame with a knowledge gained from playing through games using these openings right to the last move. These variations, six, seven or even ten moves long, are hopelessly inadequate in themselves.

Pirc Defence

If White starts **1 e4 d6 2 d4** Black could well interpose **2 . . . ♘f6** immediately—it cuts down White's possibilities—and then on 3 ♘c3 to continue 3 . . . g6 (diag 229). White has several possible plans here. 4 f4 ♗g7 ♘f3 is the popular Austrian Attack. After 5 . . . 0–0 it can take several forms: one is 6 e5 ♘fd7; another 6 ♗e2 c5 7 dc ♕a5 (threatening . . . ♘xe4) and a third way is 6 ♗d3 ♘c6.

A more solid continuation for White is 4 ♘f3 ♗g7 5 ♗e2 0–0 6 0–0 when Black can try 6 . . . ♗g4 or, with a similar objective, 6 . . . ♘c6.

Black has to treat White's plan 4 ♗c4 ♗g7 5 ♕e2 with extreme care. This sharp variation is recommended to round off your repertoire when you're White, p. 118. Perhaps best is 5 . . . c6.

Avoid routine thinking even if you adopt a universal defence. In postal chess players try to cut down on postage and time by sending 'conditional' moves; for instance they are used for obvious recaptures. In one particular game, White posted off his score sheet 1 d4. What happened was told by the player who had Black. He saved a lot of postage by replying 1 . . . g6 and pencilled in the conditional 'any', meaning any move by White, 2 . . . ♗g7. When the score-sheet came back inked in 2 ♗h6 ♗g7 3 ♗xg7, he, having lost a bishop, and faced with the loss of a rook, gracefully resigned.

Benoni or Benko Gambit

There's another defence that could well be built into a repertoire for Black. This is the Benoni Gambit (or as the Americans call it, the Benko Gambit) against the Queen's Pawn Opening. It goes 1 d4 ♘f6 2 c4 c5 3 d5 b5 4 cb a6 5 ba ♗xa6 (diag 230). Black wants to have pressure along the two open files and to use that as a way of turning White's position. Black would envisage a position something like diagram 231. See the co-ordination between the rook at b8 and the finachettoed bishop at g7 against White's b2 pawn; that could hold up the development of White's bishop at c1 and the rook at a1. The black knight f6 is no fixture; the other knight at d7 —one imagines a possible post at d3, realised by . . . c4 and . . . ♘c5;

other plans for the knight include going via d7 and b6 to c4 or a4, or even the journey ♘b8–a6–c7–b5–d4. The queen usually has no fixed post—it would be placed on any of a5, b6 or c7. That's a good jumping off position for the pieces. I think the gambit is very good. I've no qualms about playing it.

But what is a suitable opening for a similar attitude if White plays 1 e4? In queen side operations from the Benoni Gambit, the black king position is not at high risk, but gambits on the other wing (like e4 e5 2 ♘f3 f5!?) particularly expose the king. Black's best counter-attacking defence is generally thought to be the Sicilian.

One can play the Sicilian with **1 e4 c5 2 ♘f3** then **2 . . . g6**. If White plays the normal sort of plan (3 d4) Black could continue development and pressure (3 . . . ♗g7) as 4 dc can be coped with by 4 . . . ♕a5+.

Or you could try to master the Sicilian Dragon Variation: **1 e4 c5 2 ♘f3 d6 3 d4 cd 4 ♘xd4 ♘f6 5 ♘c3 g6.**

230
W

231

WHEN WHITE—(A Serious Repertoire)

Let's imagine you are preparing openings for very serious competitions. When White, you decide to continue with 1 e4 which you think fits your image. Nowadays you expect to meet 1 . . . e5 or 1 . . . c5 most often. You'll need therefore to study them in some depth. Less usual moves are: 1 . . . g6; 1 . . . d6; 1 . . . ♘f6; 1 . . . e6; 1 . . . d5; 1 . . . c6 and even 1 . . . ♘c6; they will all require some attention.

The King's Gambit

After **1 e4 e5** I strongly want to recommend the King's Gambit **2 f4** (diag 232).

It's an ancient opening which has not been very popular. But I estimate that it is due for a revival. Among those who have played it in recent years are Spassky, Bronstein, Korchnoi, Keres, Planinc,

Basman. . . . Fischer made a determined effort in 1960–61 to refute the opening before adopting it himself. White sacrifices a pawn to free the centre for his own pawns and pieces. There is a prospect for early castling and targets for the rook along the f-file. It has the additional psychological advantage that lots of opponents will under-estimate its true qualities through the years of neglect. The opening leads to lively yet unclear positions in which White has as prolonged an initiative as in the more popular Ruy Lopez (1 e4 e5 2 ♘f3 ♘c6 3 ♗b5).

I am giving you an expert repertoire based on the King's Gambit. 1 e4 e5 2 f4. Black can reply 2 . . . ef (accepting the gambit pawn); 2 . . . d5!? (Falkbeer's Counter-Gambit); 2 . . . ♘f6 and 2 . . . ♕h4+ —both counter-attacking; and decline the gambit with 2 . . . ♗c5 and 2 . . . d6. Some details on each line follows.

KING'S GAMBIT ACCEPTED

After 2 . . . ef 3 ♘f3! Black has a) 3 . . . g5, b) 3 . . . h6, c) 3 . . . d6, d) 3 . . . ♘f6, e) 3 . . . d5 and f) 3 . . . ♗e7.

   a) 3 . . . g5 4 h4 g4 5 ♘e5!

This is the Kieseritsky Gambit. Akiba Rubinstein, one of the greatest positional players of the early years of this century, spent years analysing the complications of this variation in the belief that White should win. His judgement seems sound.

   5 . . . ♗g7! (diag 233) From a wide choice, which include 5 . . . d5, 5 . . . ♘f6 and 5 . . . h5, this is probably best.

232
B

233
W

   6 d4 ♘f6   7 ♘c3 d6   8 ♘d3 0–0   9 ♘xf4 ♘xe4   10 ♘xe4 ♖e8 11 ♔f2 ♖xe4   12 c3 ♔xf6! Not prepared to retreat 13 g3 ♗h6   14 ♗d3 ♗xf4   15 ♗xf4 ♖xf4+   16 gf ♕xf4+   17 ♔e2!! g3   18 ♕d2! ♗g4+   19 ♔e1 with a tense position which should go in White's favour as Black's knight and rook are still out of play, e.g. 19 . . . ♕f3   20 ♖f1 g2   21 ♖xf3 g1=♕+   22 ♖f1.

If you obtain a game which leads into this particular variation, don't expect it will follow automatically through to move 22. Therefore study each move and try to determine the reasons for it being played and wherein lay the choice. Play through Kieseritsky Gambit games as you find them and add their ideas to your background knowledge.

Never accept the recommended moves of opening books as complete gospel. Their lines are being constantly subjected to change and improvement.

b) 3 . . . h6

4 d4 g5 5 h4 ♗g7 6 g3 g4 7 ♘h2 fg 8 ♘xg4 d6 9 c3 ♘f6 10 ♘xf6+ ♛xf6 11 ♗e3 ♘c6 12 ♘d2 ♗d7 13 ♛b3 0–0–0 14 0–0–0.

Though White remains a pawn down, his pieces are very active. This more than compensates him for the material deficit.

c) 3 . . . d6

Bobby Fischer's line. He tried to refute the King's Gambit with this move in 1961. His follow-up enables Black to avoid the Kieseritsky and other conventional ideas. However, White can play a restrained continuation, not analysed in Fischer's article.

4 d3 g5 5 h4 g4 6 ♘g1! (diag 234)

Note that White is not dogmatic in his play with this piece. In the Kieseritsky it went to e5, in the second variation it retreated to h2; g1 is a third possibility. In other variations ♘g5 is utilised.

6 . . . ♗h6 7 ♗d2 ♘c6 8 ♘c3 ♗e6 9 ♘ce2! In this case White wins back the pawn with a good game. White's overall plan has been to hold back his centre in order to avoid premature pawn exchanges.

d) 3 . . . ♘f6

4 e5 ♘h5 5 ♛e2 This is played to discourage Black's . . . d6 or . . . d5. 5 . . . ♗e7 6 d4 0–0 6 . . . ♗h4+ would prove a waste of time. 7 ♘c3 d6 8 ♗d2 de 9 de ♗h4+ 10 g3 fg 11 0–0–0 ♗d7 12 hg ♘xg3 13 ♛h2. All this happened in a game won by the British master, Michael Basman, a few years ago. White has lots of open lines on to Black's king position.

e) 3 . . . d5

4 ed ♘f6 5 ♗b5+ 5 ♘c3 ♗d6 might also turn out a little better for White. 5 . . . c6 6 dc ♘xc6!? 7 d4 ♗d6 8 0–0 This improves upon White's play in the game Hartston–Spassky, from the 1965–66 Hastings tournament, 8 . . . 0–0 9 c3 ♗g4 10 ♘bd2 ♘d5 11 ♘c4 ♗c7 12 ♛d3

White's central control gives him the better of it.

f) 3 . . . ♗e7

4 ♗e2 (diag 235) This is the newest research idea here! 4 . . . ♘f6 After 4 . . . ♗h4+ 5 ♔f1 ♗e7 it's difficult to know whether White's unhappy king position fully justifies the waste of time. Now 6 d4 g5

7 ♘e5 h5 8 ♗c4 would give White excellent play. **5 ♘c3 d5 6 ed ♘xd5 7 ♘xd5 8 d4 g5 9 0–0** and White has lots of attacking chances.

FALKBEER'S COUNTER-GAMBIT
2 . . . d5!? (diag 236)

This is the Falkbeer Counter-Gambit, which tries to show that White's f4 move was wasteful. **3 ed e4!? 4 d3 ♘f6 5 de!** Most masters now believe this to be White's best continuation against the Falkbeer. Play could well continue **5 . . . ♘xe4 6 ♘f3 ♗c5 7 ♕e2 ♗f5 8 ♘c3 ♕e7 9 ♗e3 ♗xe3 10 ♕xe3 ♘xc3 11 ♕xe7+ ♔xe7 12 bc** with serious difficulties for Black.

COUNTER-ATTACK BY 2 . . . ♘f6 AND 2 . . . ♕h4+
2 . . . ♘f6

This little known method of defence, which I used in a game with Fischer in 1968, can take a lot of the sting out of the gambit; that the game went **3 fe ♘xe4 4 ♘f3 ♘g5 5 d4** (White could try 5 c3, with a slower build-up.) **5 . . . ♘xf3+ 6 ♕xf3 ♕h4+ 7 ♕f2 ♕xf2+ 8 ♔xf2 ♘c6 9 c3 d6.**

2 . . . ♕h4+!?
3 g3 ♕e7 Ray Keene, the 1971 British Champion, has been experimenting with this idea, which is intended to weaken the White king's likely refuge. If **4 fe d6! 5 ed ♕xe4+.**

GAMBIT DECLINED 2 . . . ♗c5 AND 2 . . . d6
2 . . . ♗c5!
An old, reliable way of declining the gambit. If now 3 fe, White will find **3 . . . ♕h4+** awkward. **3 ♘f3 d6 4 ♗c4 4 c3** is another plan. **4 . . . ♘f6 5 ♘c3 ♘c6 6 d3** when Black's best move is **6 . . . a6!** (diag 237), to keep the embarrassing bishop that prevents White's 0–0; but White remains with lots of chances.

2 . . . d6
Against this quiet move, White can build up pressure; **3 ♘f3 ♘f6**

4 ♘c3 ♘c6 5 ♗b5 ♗d7 6 d3 e5xf4 7 ♗xf4 with 0–0 to follow, when the rook comes to a good open file.

SPASSKY–BRONSTEIN
As an illustration of the lively character of the King's Gambit, here is the game Spassky–Bronstein, played at Leningrad in 1960: 1 e4 e5 2 f4 ef 3 ♘f3 d5 4 ed ♗d6 5 ♘c3 ♘e7 6 d4 0–0 7 ♗d3 ♘d7 8 0–0 h6? (*8 . . . ♘g6 and 8 . . . ♘f6 are better.*) 9 ♘e4 ♘xd5 10 c4 ♘e3 11 ♗xe3 fe 12 c5 ♗e7 13 ♗c2! ♖e8 14 ♕d3 e2 15 ♘d6! ♘f8? (*Leads to a loss. Spassky suggested 15 . . . ♗xd6, upon which there could follow 16 ♕h7+ ♔f8 17 cd ef=♕+ 18 ♖xf1 cd 19 ♕h8+ ♔e7 20 ♖e1+ ♘e5 21 ♕xg7 ♖g8 22 ♕xh6 ♕b6 23 ♔h1 ♗e6 24 de d5, as a possible line of defence.*) 16 ♘xf7! ef=♕+ 17 ♖xf1 ♗f5 (*if 17 . . . ♔xf7 18 ♘e5++ and mates, or 17 . . . ♕d5 18 ♘3e5 should win.*) 18 ♕xf5 ♕d7 19 ♕f4 ♗f6 20 ♘3e5 ♕e7 21 ♗b3 ♗xe5 22 ♘xe5+ ♔h7 23 ♕e4+ and Black resigned.

Against the Sicilian
The Sicilian Defence, reached after **1 e4 c5**, is contemporarily the most popular defence to White's king pawn opening. The best way of tackling it is to play into the main variations with 2 ♘f3 followed by 3 d4 cd ♘xd4, but there is a tremendous amount of knowledge that you may feel obliged to acquire.

Therefore against the Sicilian I am recommending that readers adopt the Morra Gambit **2 d4 cd 3 c3** (diag 238). This originated in the last century, was forgotten, and then resuscitated in the 1950's by the Yugoslav grandmaster, Milan Matulovic.

White sacrifices a pawn for quick development of the pieces. Matulovic won many short games with it. If Black defends ably and White continues in the correct spirit, Black can obtain at best a position with about level chances. A typical first phase development plan for White after the gambit is accepted (3 . . . dc 4 ♘xc3) is shown in diagram 239.

After 1 e4 c5   2 d4 dc   3 c3, what replies can Black consider? There is the gambit accepted by 3 . . . dc   4 ♘xc3, or two important ways of declining—3 . . . ♘f6 and 3 . . . d5.

MORRA GAMBIT ACCEPTED

After **1 e4 c5   2 d4 cd   3 c3 dc   4 ♘xc3 ♘c6   5 ♘f3** Black has four main plans of development—a) 5 . . . g6, b) 5 . . . e5, c) 5 . . . e6, d) 5 . . . d6.

a) **5 . . . g6**

6 ♗c4 ♗g7   7 e5! (diag 240)

This disruptive pawn thrust gives White a fierce attack; two samples—7 . . . ♗xe5   8 ♗xf7+ ♔xf7   9 ♘xe5+ ♘xe5   10 ♕d5+ and takes the knight, unless Black is foolhardy enough to advance his king into gravest danger; after 7 . . . ♕a5   8 0–0 ♘xe5   9 ♘xe5 ♗xe5   10 ♘d5 e6   11 ♖e1 is very promising for White—if, say, 11 . . . f6 White plays 12 ♗b3 (*threatening 13 f4*) 12 . . . ♔f7   13 ♖xe5 fe   14 ♕f3+ ♔e8   15 ♗h6! ♘xh6   16 ♕f6 when White threatens to mate by 17 ♕e7 or take the rook on h8.

b) **5 . . . e5**

6 ♗c4 puts Black in grave trouble, e.g. 6 . . . ♗e7?   7 ♕d5 and White has great hopes of a quick win, or 6 . . . ♗c5   7 ♗xf7+.

c) **5 . . . e6**

6 ♗c4 a6   7 ♕e2 b5 Black plans expansion on the queen's side. However, White can continue with his basic developing plan. **8 ♗b3 d6   9 0–0 ♗e7   10 ♖d1 ♕c7   11 ♗f4 ♗b7   12 ♖ac1 ♕b8   13 e5 d5   14 ♗xd5 ed   15 ♘xd5** when White threatens 16 e6, with a strong attack.

d) **5 . . . d6**

6 ♗c4 (diag 241) **6 . . . e6** This is Black's most stable system.

Black can also try:

1) 6 . . . ♘f6?!   7 e5 de (diag 242. *In a game at the 1973 Junior World Championships, Black lost his queen after 7 . . . ♘xe5?? 8 ♘xe5 de   9 ♗xf7+.*) 8 ♕xd8+ ♔xd8 (*Another illustrative game—*

8 . . . ♔xd8　9 ♘g5 ♔c7?!　10 ♘xf7 ♖g8　11 ♘b5+ ♔b8　12 ♘xe5
♘xe5　13 ♗f4 ♘fd7　14 ♗xg8 a6　15 ♘d4 ♔a7　16 0—0 *Black resigned.*) 9 ♘b5 ♖b8　10 ♘xe5 e6　11 ♘c7+ ♔e7　12 ♗e3 and White
threatens 13 ♗c5; White's strong initiative, properly exploited,
should yield a win.

2) 6 . . . a6 (*as played by two grandmasters at the strong San
Antonio, Texas, tournament of 1972; Ken Smith, the American
master played—rather routinely—7 0—0. He would have done better
to follow a recommendation from Moscow's Central Chess Club
bulletin, with . . .*) 7 e5 de (*If 7 . . . e6　8 ♗g5*) 8 ♕xd8+ ♘xd8
(*Or 8 . . . ♔xd8　9 ♘g5 ♘h6　10 ♗xf7*) 9 ♘d5! with threats; one line
from Moscow leads on from 9 . . . ♘e6　10 ♘b6 ♖b8　11 ♘xe5 ♘f6
to the startling 12 ♘xf7! ♔xf7　13 ♗f4 with a nice position to have.

7 0—0 (Diag 243) when again I append examples of play:

1) 7 . . . ♘ge7　8 ♗g5 a6 (*If 8 . . . h6　9 ♘b5!*) 9 ♕e2 h6　10 ♗e3
♗d7　11 ♖ad1 ♘g6 when White can play 12 ♘d4 planning f2—f4—
f5.

2) 7 . . . ♘f6　8 ♕e2 a6　9 ♖d1 ♕c7　10 ♗f4 ♘e5　11 ♗xe5 de　12
♖ac1 ♗d7 (*On 12 . . . ♕b8　13 ♗ b5+! gives White a strong attack.*)

13 ♗xe6 ♗xe6 14 ♘d5 ♕b8 15 ♘c7+ ♔e7 16 ♕d2 ♘e8 17 ♘xe6 fe
18 ♕d7+ ♔f6 19 ♘g5 ♔xg5 20 ♕xe6 ♘f6 21 ♕f5+ ♔h6 22 ♖c3
♕e8 (*Or 22 . . . ♘h5 23 ♖h3 g6 24 ♖xh5 gh 25 ♕f6 mate*) 23 ♖h3+
♔h5 24 g4 ♕xh3 25 g5+ ♔h5 26 ♕xh3+ ♔xg5 27 ♕f5+ ♔h6
28 ♖d3 ♘h5 29 ♖h3 g6 30 ♖xh5+ ♔g7 31 ♔xe5+ and White's
material advantage should enable him to win.

3) 7 . . . ♘f6 8 ♕e2 ♗e7 9 ♖d1 (Threat *e5*) 9 . . . e5! (*Best;
If 9 . . . ♗d7 10 ♗g5 0–0 11 ♗xf6 gf! 12 ♘b5 ♕b8 13 ♖d3
a6? 14 ♘xd6! with a continuing initiative.*) 10 h3! (*White's enduring
advantage is through the greater scope of his pieces; it's worthwhile
to prevent . . . ♗g4.*) 10 . . . 0–0 11 b3 a6 12 ♗a3 ♕a5 13 ♕b2
♘b4 14 ♖ac1 b5 15 ♗xb4 ♕xb4 16 ♘d5 ♘xd5 17 ♗xd5 ♖a7
when White's pieces are much better co-ordinated. Now he can
prepare by 18 ♖c2 to double on the c-file.

4) 7 . . . a6 8 ♕e2 ♗e7 9 ♖d1 ♗d7 (Diag. 244) is an order of moves
causing concern at the time of writing. Where is White to develop his
c1-bishop? Black has held back from . . . ♘f6 in order to avoid White's
♗g5. 10 ♗f4 would encourage Black to play 10 . . . e5 11 ♗e3 ♗g4
with activity that casts doubt on the sufficiency of White's pawn
sacrifice. Perhaps White should postpone the decision and play 10 h3
and after 10 . . . ♘f6 11 ♗g5 0–0 12 ♗xf6 gf! look into attacking
possibilities based on e4–e5 or restraining Black's pieces by 13 a4.

The position at diagram 245, after 12 . . . gf, is psychologically
interesting. If, on taking the white side of the position, you feel that
you are a pawn down and that you are desperately trying to regain
it and re-establish a balance, then you should not be playing gambit
openings. If, however, you naturally contrast the power and possibil-

244
B

245
W

ities of the white pieces with those of Black's, and feel that you can make something of it, then you can play this opening.

MORRA GAMBIT DECLINED

After **1 e4 c5 2 d4 cd 3 c3** Black can decline the gambit by 3 . . . ♘f6 and 3 . . . d5, e.g.

3 . . . ♘f6

This is the usual reaction from opponents who are suddenly confronted with the Morra Gambit. **4 e5 ♘d5 5 ♗c4 ♕c7!** (If 5 . . . ♘b6 6 ♗b3 or 5 . . . e6 6 d4) **6 ♕e2 ♘b6 7 ♗b3** (Also possible is 7 ♗d3.) **7 . . . d3!? 8 ♕xd3 ♘a6 9 ♗e3 ♘c5 10 ♗xc5 ♕xc5 11 ♘f3** with White having a reasonable position. Black cannot save his advanced pawn.

3 . . . d5

when a game played by former champion, Alexander Alekhine, can serve as a model for White.

4 ed ♕xd5 5 cd ♘c6 6 ♘f3 ♗g4 7 ♗e2 e6 8 ♘c3 ♗b4 9 0–0 ♕a5 10 a3 (diag 246).

Now Black should play 10 . . . ♗xc3 11 bc ♘f6; instead he gave Alekhine the opportunity to carry out a vigorous attack against the uncastled black king.

10 . . . ♘f6 11 d5!! ed 12 ab! ♕xa1 13 ♘d2 This threatens to net the black queen by 14 ♘b3. **13 . . . ♗xe2 14 ♕xe2+ ♘e7 15 ♖e1 0–0 16 ♘b3 ♕a6 17 ♕xa6 ba 18 ♖xe7**

White has a material and positional advantage and duly won; Alekhine–Podgorny, Prague 1943.

Other Defences to 1 e2–e4

I give one short line of play as a sample, against each of the less likely defences that you may encounter.

PIRC DEFENCE

After **1 e4 d6 2 d4 ♘f6** White could adopt the system **3 ♘c3 g6 4 ♗c4 ♗g7 5 ♕e2** as the opening 'theorists' are divided over what is a sufficient reply for Black.

KING'S FIANCHETTO DEFENCE

Against this 'modern' defence **1 e4 g6** White can continue **2 d4 ♗g7 3 c3** and later f4.

ALEKHINE'S DEFENCE

Against this (**1 e4 ♘f6**) you could try the unusual line **2 e5 ♘d5 3 ♗c4 ♘b6 4 ♗b3 d6 5 d4 ed 6 ♕h5**, threatening mate, but don't be upset if it doesn't come off, you'll still have a reasonable game.

FRENCH DEFENCE

This is **1 e4 e6** (the beginner's plan—see p. 64). I would follow up 2 d4 d5 3 ♘c3 and whether my opponent chooses the classical line 3 . . . ♘f6 or goes into the knotty Winawer Variation, 3 . . . ♗b4, then continue with the straightforward old-fashioned bishop development 4 ♗d3.

CENTRE COUNTER

If your opponent should play it (**1 e4 d5**), take the pawn (2 ed); if the queen recaptures (2 . . . ♕xd5) White faces no severe opening problems after 3 ♘c3 followed by 4 d4. When the recapture, possible on move 2, is delayed by 2 . . . ♘f6, don't try to hold on to the pawn but play 3 d4 ♘xd5 4 ♘f3.

CARO-KANN DEFENCE

This (**1 e4 c6**) has been a favourite of three world champions. Though not active in appearance it must not be treated disdainfully. Spassky, when trying to wrest the world championship title from Petrosian used the line 2 d4 d5 3 ♘c3 de 4 ♘xe4 ♗f5 5 ♘g3 ♗g6 (diag 247) 6 h4 h6 7 ♘f3 ♘d7 8 h5 ♗h7 9 ♗d3 ♗xd3 10 ♕xd3 ♕c7 11 ♗d2 e6 12 ♕e2 ♘gf6 13 0–0–0 0–0–0 14 ♘e5 with pressure.

NIMZOWITSCH'S DEFENCE

This (**1 e4 ♘c6**) is very rarely played. I'm giving it in detail only because readers might like to use it, when Black, as a surprise weapon. The recommended reply is 2 d4 d5 3 ♘c3 de 4 d5 ♘b8 5 ♗f4 ♘f6 6 ♗c4 c6 7 ♘ge2 cd 8 ♘xd5, but many players after Black's 4 . . . ♘b8 will begin to treat the position casually; and that can be a fatal mistake. Black has another way of handling the defence after 1 e4 ♘c6 2 d4 by 2 . . . e5 3 de ♘xe5 4 f4 ♘g6 (diag 248); Black threatens . . . ♗c5 commanding the c5–g1 diagonal; White should get there first by 5 ♗e3, when there could follow 5 . . . ♗b4+ 6 c3 ♗a5 with an unclear position—maybe Black is okay.

From this repertoire one goes on over the months building up a more detailed network acquired by personal experience and from the study of master games. If you are ambitious you will want to master the problems and intricacies of your chosen lines and hope thereby to control the direction of play.

But do not rely on opening knowledge to bring you more than partial success. Against real chessplayers it will not alone suffice.

If you are one of those who constantly varies your openings you will be entertained by a wide range of positions. But you must occasionally expect to be at the receiving end of unpleasant shocks and forced to work hard and consume a lot of time trying to survive.

Finally there is an argument for changing one's repertoire every year or two in order to combat staleness and routine if so affected.

7 Great players, games and positions

The first international chess event on record was held at Madrid in 1574 on the occasion of the visit of the Calabrian (Italian), Giovanni Leonardo, who beat the two best Spanish players, Ruy Lopez and Ceron, in the presence of King Philip II.

Philidor
André Philidor (1726–1795), a French musical composer (23 operas), was the first great master of the chessboard whose talent we can measure in the only acceptable way by an examination of the records of his games. (See also comment on Philidor, p. 76).

Here is one of two blindfold simultaneous games played in London in 1783. White: **Count Brühl**, Black **Philidor**. 1 e4 e5 2 ♗c4 c6 3 ♕e2 d6 4 c3 f5 5 d3 ♘f6 6 ef ♗xf5 7 d4 e4 8 ♗g5 d5 9 ♗b3 ♗d6 10 ♘d2 ♘bd7 11 h3 h6 12 ♗e3 ♕e7 13 f4? (*Imprisoning his own dark-squared bishop*) 13 . . . h5! 14 c4 a6 15 cd cd 16 ♕f2 0–0 17 ♘e2 b5 18 0–0 ♘b6 19 ♘g3 g6 20 ♖ac1 ♘c4 21 ♘xf5 gf 22 ♕g3+ ♔g7! 23 ♕xg7+ ♔xg7 24 ♗xc4 bc 25 g3 ♖ab8 26 b3 ♗a3 27 ♖c2 cb 28 ab (*28 ♘xb3 was better*) 28 . . . ♖fc8 29 ♖xc8 ♖xc8 30 ♖a1 ♗b4 31 ♖xa6 ♖c3 32 ♔f2 ♖d3 33 ♖a2 ♗xd2 34 ♖xd2 ♖xb3 35 ♖c2 h4! (diag 249) 36 ♖c7+ ♔g6 37 gh ♘xh5 38 ♖d7 ♘xf4 39 ♗xf4 ♖f3+ 40 ♔g2 ♖xf4 41 ♖xd5 ♖f3 42 ♖d8 ♖d3 43 d5 f4 44 d6 ♖d2+ 45 ♔f1 ♔f7! 46 h5 e3 47 h6 f3 White resigned. Black mates or queens first.

Sarratt, La Bourdonnais and Staunton
The first great British player was J. H. Sarratt, who won renown as a master of real attacking ability, a codifier of rules and a writer (Treatise–1808 and New Treatise–posthumously in 1821). The centre of world chess during the nineteenth-century veered between Paris and London, with North America coming into the picture in the 1880s and '90s. A famous series of matches between Louis Charles Mahé de la Bourdonnais (1795-1840) of France and Alexander MacDonnell (born Belfast, 1798-1835) at the Westminster Club in 1834 resulted in wins for the Frenchman 16-5 (with 4 draws) followed by 28-22 (9 draws). The prestige balance switched

back to England when Howard Staunton (1810–74) met Pierre Charles Fournier de Saint-Amant (1800–72) at the Cercle d'Echecs, Paris in 1843 and was the victor by 11 wins, six losses and 4 drawn.

La Bourdonnais–MacDonnell, game 17; Queen's Gambit Accepted—1 d4 d5 2 c4 dc 3 e3 e5! 4 ♗xc4 ed 5 ed ♘f6 6 ♘c3 ♗e7 7 ♘f3 0–0 8 ♗e3 c6 9 h3! (*White, with a reasonable mobilisation of pieces, is justified in depriving Black of a good square for the bishop and knight.*) 9 . . . ♘bd7 10 ♗b3 ♘b6 11 0–0 ♘fd5 12 a4 a5 13 ♘e5 ♗e6 14 ♗c2 f5?! 15 ♕e2 f4 16 ♗d2 ♕e8 17 ♖ae1 ♗f7 18 ♕e4 g6 19 ♗xf4! ♘xf4 20 ♕xf4 ♗c4 (diag 250) 21 ♕h6! ♗xf1 22 ♗xg6 hg 23 ♘xg6 ♘c8 (*23 . . . ♗f6!?*) 24 ♕h8+ ♔f7 25 ♕h7+ ♔f6 26 ♘f4! ♗d3 27 ♖e6+ ♔g5 28 ♕h6+ ♔f5 29 g4 mate.

Anderssen

The first big international tournament was staged in London in 1851, the year of the 'Great Exhibition of Art and Industry' at the Crystal Palace; it was a knock-out even with 16 players; the German player Adolf Anderssen (1818–79) beat Staunton in the semi-final 4–1 and Marmeduke Wyvill in the final by 4–2. Diagram 179 shows the position from which Anderssen won the 'evergreen' game in 1852.

The 'immortal game' is how **Anderssen–Kieseritsky**, London 1851 is designated—it went 1 e4 e5 2 f4 ef 3 ♗c4 ♕h4+ 4 ♔f1 b5 5 ♗xb5 ♘f6 6 ♘f3 ♕h6 7 d3 ♘h5 8 ♘h4 ♕g5 9 ♘f5 c6? (*9 . . . g6!*) 10 ♖g1! cb 11 g4 ♘f6 12 h4 ♕g6 13 h5 ♕g5 14 ♕f3 ♘g8 15 ♗xf4 ♕f6 16 ♘c3 ♗c5 17 ♘d5 ♕xb2 (diag 251) 18 ♗d6!!? (*18 ♗e3! ♕xa1+ 19 ♔g2 ♕xg1+ 20 ♗xg1 leaves Black no defence.*) 18 . . . ♗xg1 (*Better 18 . . . ♕xa1+ 19 ♔e2 ♕b2!*) 19 e5!! Sacrificing two rooks in order to construct a mating net. 19 . . . ♕xa1+ 20 ♔e2 (*Threat is 21 ♘xg7+ ♔d8 22 ♗c7 mate.*) 20 . . . ♘a6 21 ♘xg7+ ♔d8 22 ♕f6+! ♘xf6 23 ♗e7 mate.

Morphy

Paul Morphy (1837–84) is the first great American player. Phenomenon is a better description. In the course of two years he rose to dominate the chess world as a player, to add a new dimension to chess thinking and to retire back to obscurity in New Orleans. Morphy won the first American congress in 1857 and sailed to Europe intent on toppling Staunton from a throne which the Englishman, no longer physically fit, did not want to occupy. The American convincingly established his superiority; at the end of 1858 in Paris he beat Anderssen 7–2, 2 drawn. Staunton evaded a serious contest, and, in doing so, added unknowingly to the onset of the persecution complex and melancholia that was to afflict Morphy in his later years.

Morphy–Löwenthal, match, London 1858: 1 e4 e5 2 ♘f3 ♘c6 3 ♗b5 a6 4 ♗a4 ♘f6 5 d4 ed 6 e5 ♘e4 7 0–0 ♗c5 8 ♗xc6 dc 9 ♘xd4 ♘e6?! 10 ♘xe6 ♗xe6 11 ♕e2 ♗c5 12 ♘c3 ♕e7 13 ♘e4 h6 14 ♗e3! (*To control the g1–a7 diagonal and have the possibility of f2–f4– f5*) 14 . . . ♗xe3 15 ♕xe3 ♗f5? (*15 0–0!*) 16 ♘g3 ♗xc2? 17 f4 g6 (diag 252) 18 e6! (*Threatening 19 ♕c3 attacking bishop*

251
W

252
W

and rook. If now 18 . . . 0–0–0 19 ♕a7.) 18 . . . ♗f5 19 ♘xf5 gf
20 ef+ ♔xf7 21 ♕h3 ♕f6 22 ♖ae1 ♖he8 23 ♖e5! ♔g6 24 ♖fe1
♖xe5 25 ♖xe5 ♖d8 26 ♕g3+ ♔h7 (*Black has problems as his king
has less shelter available.*) 27 h3 ♖d7 28 ♕e3 b6 29 ♔h2 c5 30 ♕e2
♕g6 31 ♖e6 ♕g7 32 ♕h5 ♖d5 (*If 32 . . . ♖f7 33 ♖xh6+.*) 33 b3 b5
(*Or 33 . . . a5 34 a4*) 34 ♖xa6 ♖d6 35 ♕xf5+ ♕g6 36 ♕xg6+ ♔xg6
37 ♖a5 ♖b6 38 g4 c6 39 ♔g3 h5 40 ♖a7 hg 41 hg ♔f6 42 f5 ♔e5
43 ♖e7+ ♔d6 44 f6 ♖b8 45 g5 ♖f8 46 ♔f4 c4 47 bc bc 48 ♔f5
c3 49 ♖e3 Black resigned (*If 49 . . . c2 50 ♖d3+ ♔c7 51 ♖c3
followed by advancing the connected passed pawns.*)

Steinitz

Wilhelm Steinitz, (1836–1900), from Bohemia, beat Anderssen in
1866 (8 wins, six losses, no draws!) and for the next 28 years can
be regarded as the world's leading player. The match in 1886 between Steinitz and Johannes Hermann Zukertort (1842–88, who was
born in Poland) is the first to be generally recognised as being for the
world championship title. It was a fluctuating event. After five
games in New York Zukertort led by four wins to one; Steinitz won
four and drew one of the St. Louis phase to gain an overall lead
5½–4½; in the final phase at New Orleans Zukertort became ex-
hausted and Steinitz won by 10–5, 5 draws.

One of the great games of the last century was **Steinitz's** win over
von Bardeleben at Hastings in 1895. Steinitz had lost a match with
Emanuel Lasker for the world title the previous year.)

Steinitz was White: 1 e2–e4 e7–e5 2 ♘g1–f3 ♘b8–c6 3 ♗f1–
c4 ♗f8–c5 4 c2–c3 ♘g8–f6 5 d2–d4. White is hoping to set up a
pawn centre that will be both aggressive and cramping. 5 . . . e5xd4
6 c3xd4 ♗c5–b4+ 7 ♘b1–c3. See p. 90 for more on these variations. 7 . . . d7–d5 Bardeleben wanted to exchange off one of the
centre pawns. 8 e4xd5 ♘f6xd5 9 0–0 Steinitz was aiming to mobil-
ise the pieces quickly. If White were to play 9 ♗xd5 instead, Black
could safely recapture 9 . . . ♕xd5. 9 . . . ♗c8–e6 10 ♗c1–g5
♗b4–e7.

Interest has re-awakened recently in this game through the
attempts of some Russian analysts to explore in depth the possibilities of this famous brilliancy. Now Steinitz embarked on a series
of exchanges of the pieces covering Black's king with a view to
bringing the rooks to bear on it. 11 ♗c4xd5 ♗e6xd5 (diag 253)
12 ♘c3xd5 The Russians have been looking at the similar idea
12 ♗xe7 ♘xe7 13 ♖e1, but it's not certain that it's an improvement.
12 . . . ♕d8xd5 13 ♗g5xe7 ♘c6xe7 There is some argument for
Black to consider recapturing with the king, viz. 13 . . . ♔xe7!?
14 ♖e1+ ♔f8 and if 15 ♕e2, then 15 . . . g6 intending 16 . . . ♔g7

and 17 . . . ♖he8. **14 ♖fe1 f7–f6** (diag 254) Bardeleben would like
to have followed this up with . . . ♔f7 and then ♘d5. **15 ♕d1–e2**

The Russians have also been investigating 15 ♕a4+!? ♔f7 16
♖ac1; now best seems 16 . . . ♕d6, planning to put the knight on
d5, where it would act as an anchor for Black's position. They
haven't come up with any line offering White clear prospects of an
advantage, but all their efforts add perspective to the original game
and show its true quality.

One line of theirs, that friends of mine have been examining in
detail, runs 15 ♕a4+ ♔f7 16 ♖ac1 c6 17 ♖xe7+ ♔xe7 18 ♕b4+
♔f7 19 ♕xb7+ ♔g6 when the Russian analysis went 20 ♖xc6–that
threatens to win Black's queen by moving the rook again, this time
with check–but after 20 . . . ♖hc8, I couldn't find more than a
draw through the knight perpetually checking, White having to
watch his back rank. But, seeking an improvement we looked at
20 ♘e5+! first, and only after 20 . . . fe to play the rook move
21 ♖xc6+–this time more effectively as it is check–and with a
further check available, White seems then to win.

The actual game continued **15 . . . ♕d5–d7** (diag 255); mate is
stopped.

Another Russian probe here. They think that nothing seems to
come from 16 d5, trying to force open the central files. But, para-
doxically, 16 ♖ad1!, hiding the rook behind the pawn, has points.
A sample line (*16 . . . ♔f7 17 ♕c4+ ♘d5 18 ♘e5+*), forces open
lines after 18 . . . fxe5 19 dxe5 and threatens both e6+ and ♖xd5.

Again the game–**16 ♖a1–c1** (diag 256) **16 . . . c7–c6** This
attempt to solidify the position is probably the decisive error. It
was pointed out in the tournament book published just after the
1895 congress, that Black could hold the position by 16 . . . ♔f7!
and, if 17 ♕xe7+ ♕xe7 18 ♖xe7+ ♔xe7 19 ♖xc7+, Black could
defend his second rank by 19 . . . ♔d6 followed by 20 ♖hc8 (threatening mate) and eventually 21 . . . ♖c7. After 16 . . . ♔f7 the Russ-

255
W

256
B

ians have looked into 17 ᗡe5+ and 17 ᗡg5+, but Black survived those attempts also.

Now let's concentrate on the game **17 d4–d5!** The d4 square is cleared to make room for the knight. **17 . . . c6xd5 18 ᗡf3–d4 ᗡe8–f7 19 ᗡd4-e6 ☖h8–c8** This stops White's rook coming to c7. **20 ♕e2–g4!** Steinitz thus threatened 21 ♕xg7+ ☖e8 22 ♕f8 checkmate. **20 . . . g7–g6 21 ᗡe6–g5+** This check uncovers an attack of queen on to queen and **21 . . . ☖f7–e8** was the only way to save the queen. Now the real attack begins! (diag 257) **22 ☖e1xe7+!** By this move, Steinitz shows a full appreciation of the tactical possibilities within the position. If 22 . . . ♕xe7 with 23 ☖xc8+ ☖xc8 24 ♕xc8+ White would have won a knight. For Black to recapture with the king would be even more disastrous—22 . . . ☖xe7 23 ☖e1+ ☖d6 24 ♕b4+ ☖c7 25 ᗡe6+—and after the forced retreat 25 . . . ☖b8 comes 26 ♕f4+ ☖c7 27 ᗡxc7 ♕xc7 28 ☖e8 mate.

Black saw this and played instead **22 . . . ☖e8–f8**; the game proceeded **23 ☖e7–f7+** Not 23 ♕xd7??—Black mates by 23 . . . ☖xc1. White must create the opportunity to take the queen with CHECK. **23 . . . ☖f8–g8** If 23 . . . ♕xf7 White again has 24 ☖xc8+. **24 ☖f7–g7+ ☖g8–h8** (diag 258) If the king had started to return by

257
W

258
W

24 . . . ♔f8 White, by 25 ♘xh7+, would ensure the win of the black queen with check.

The last move played in the game was **25 ♖xh7+**; von Bardeleben had gone from the room and didn't return! When Black's time had run out, Steinitz was awarded the game and then demonstrated the forced finish that he was intending—25 . . . ♔g8 26 ♖g7+ ♔h8 27 ♕h4+ ♔xg7 28 ♕h7+ ♔f8 29 ♕h8+ ♔e7 30 ♕g7+ ♔e8 31 ♕g8+ ♔e7 32 ♕f7+ ♔d8 (*if 32 . . . ♔d6 33 ♕xf6+ ♔e6 34 ♕xe6 MATE*) 33 ♕f8+ ♔e8 34 ♘f7+ ♔d7 35 ♕d6 MATE. Who doesn't wish he could play as well as that!

Lasker

Dr Emanuel Lasker (born Germany 1868—died New York 1941), world champion from 1894 (he beat Steinitz 10-5, 4 draws) to 1921, was the fighter, philosopher and the intellectual at the chessboard. The first game of his title defence match in 1907 with USA'S **Frank Marshall** (White) went 1 e4 e5 2 ♘f3 ♘c6 3 ♗b5 ♘f6 4 d4 ed 5 0—0 ♗e7 6 e5 ♘e4 7 ♘xd4 0—0 9 ♘f5 d5 9 ♗xc6 bc 10 ♘xe7+ ♕xe7 11 ♖e1 ♕h4 12 ♗e3 f6 13 f3 fe 14 fe d4 15 g3 (*If 15 ♗d2 ♗g4 16 ♕c1 ♖f2! 17 ♗g5 ♖xg2+ 18 ♔xg2 ♗h3+ should win.*) 15 . . . ♕f6 16 ♗xd4 ed 17 ♖f1 ♕xf1+ 18 ♕xf1 ♖xf1+ 19 ♔xf1 (diag 259) It was surprising that Lasker had allowed the queens to be exchanged. At a casual glance the position looks even, but with a fine rook manoeuvre Lasker seizes the initiative. 19 . . . ♖b8! 20 b3 ♖b5! (*Here the rook has increased attacking possibil-*

259
B

ities. If 21 ♘d2 ♖h5 22 ♔g2 ♖c5 23 ♖c1 ♗a6 hoping for . . . ♗d3.)
21 c4 ♖h5 22 ♔g1 (*On 22 h4 g5! 23 hg ♖h1+ sets up a permanent
pin along the 8th rank.*) 22 . . . c5 (*Making his third rank available
for his rook.*) 23 ♘d2 ♔f7! 24 ♖f1+ ♔e7 25 a3 ♖h6 26 h4 ♖a6
27 ♖a1 ♗g4 28 ♔f2 ♔e6 29 a4 ♔e5 30 ♔g2 ♖f6 31 ♖e1 d3
32 ♖f1 ♔d4 33 ♖xf6 gf 34 ♔f2 c6 35 a5 a6 36 ♘f1 ♔xe4 37 ♔e1
♗e2 38 ♘d2+ ♔e3 39 ♘b1 f5 40 ♘d2 h5 41 ♘b1 ♔f3 42 ♘c3
♔xg3 43 ♘a4 f4 44 ♘xc5 f3 45 ♘e4+ ♔f4 46 ♘d6 c5 47 b4 cb
48 c5 b3 49 ♘c4 ♔g3 50 ♘e3 b2 White resigned. A beautifully
played and easy to understand ending.

Capablanca
José Raoul Capablanca (1888–1942), Cuban, world champion
surprisingly for only six years (1921–27), played at the height of his
career with an effortlessness that made all wonder that he could
ever be beaten. When he took the title from Lasker in 1921 with
four wins, no losses and ten draws there was only one fleeting
instance in the whole of the match when Lasker might have gained
a substantial advantage.

Capablanca-Janowski, played at St Petersburg 1914: 1 e4 e5
2 ♘f3 ♘c6 3 ♗b5 a6 4 ♗xc6 dc 5 ♘c3 ♗c5 (*5 . . . f6 is more usual
and better.*) 6 d3 ♗g4 7 ♗e3 ♗xe3? (*7 . . . ♕e7*) 8 fe ♕e7 9 0–0
0–0–0? (*Janowski was probably unaware that he was running into
any danger. He needed to castle on the other wing after 9 . . . ♘h6.*)
10 ♕e1 ♘h6 Capablanca had an almost unerring instinct as to which
sector of the board to direct his energies as the next move shows.
11 ♖b1!! (diag 260) White's centre is solid. A wing attack is appropriate;
and Janowski can do nothing about this one. 11 . . . f6 12 b4
♘f7 13 a4 ♗xf3 14 ♖xf3 b6? (*It would have been better to play
14 . . . b5 and follow up with . . . ♔b7 and . . . ♖a8.*) 15 b5! cb 16
ab a5 17 ♘d5 ♕c5 18 c4! ♘g5 19 ♖f2! ♘e6 20 ♕c3 ♖d7 21
♖d1! ♔b7 22 d4 ♕d6 23 ♖c2 ed 24 ed ♘f4 25 c5 ♘xd5 26 ed
♕xd5 27 c6+ ♔b8 28 cd ♕xd7 29 d5 ♖e8 30 d6 cd 31 ♕c6 Black
resigned.

Capablanca-Lasker, 11th game, 1921 match: 1 d4 d5 2 ♘f3 e6
3 c4 ♘f6 4 ♗g5 ♘bd7 5 e3 ♗e7 6 ♘c3 0–0 7 ♖c1 ♖e8 8 ♕c2 c6
9 ♗d3 dc 10 ♗xc4 ♘d5 11 ♗xe7 ♖xe7? (*Better and usual is 11 . . .
♕xe7 12 0–0 ♘xc3 13 ♕xc3 e5*) 12 0–0 ♘f8 (*12 . . . ♘xc3 13
♕xc6 b6 would be more vigorous.*) 13 ♖fd1 ♗d7 14 e4 ♘b6?!
15 ♗f1 ♖c8 16 b4 (diag 261) 16 . . . ♗e8 17 ♕b3 ♖ec7 18 a4 ♘g6
19 a5 ♘d7 20 e5 (*With a post at d6 for the knight*) 20 . . . b6
21 ♘e4 ♖b8 22 ♕c3 (*22 ♕a3 would have been more exact. Black's
knight now comes to d5 with gain of tempo.*) 22 . . . ♘f4 23 ♘d6
♘d5 24 ♕a3 f6!? (*24 . . . ♕e7!?*) 25 ♘xe8 ♕xe8 26 ef gf 27 b5!
♖bc8 28 bc ♖xc6 29 ♖xc6 ♖xc6 30 ab ab 31 ♖e1 (*White's

queenside initiative has been exchanged for a weakened black king's position.) 31 . . . ♕c8 32 ♘d2 ♘f8 33 ♘e4 ♕d8 34 h4! (*Against Black's plan of 34 . . . f5, followed by 35 . . . ♖c3, Capablanca had prepared 35 ♕g3+ ♔h8 36 ♕e5+ ♔g8 37 ♗b5 ♖c7 38 ♘g5 ♖e7 39 ♗c4 ♘c7 40 h5! b5 41 ♗b3 when Black cannot cope with both d5 and ♘xe6.*) 34 . . . ♖c7?! (*Capablanca suggested 34 . . . h6, preparing . . . f5.*) 35 ♕b3 ♖g7! 36 g3 ♖a7 37 ♗c4 (*Threatening to take twice on d5.*) 37 . . . ♖a5 38 ♘c3 ♘xc3 39 ♕xc3 ♔f7 40 ♕e3 ♕d6 41 ♕e4 ♖a4?! (*41 . . . ♖a7.*) 42 ♕b7+ ♔g6 43 ♕c8 ♕b4 44 ♖c1 ♕e7 45 ♗d3+ ♔h6 46 ♖c7 ♖a1+ 47 ♔g2 ♕d6 48 ♕xf8+! Black resigned. Relentless machine-like chess with Lasker always under pressure.

Rubinstein

When Capablanca emerged after the San Sebastian tournament in 1911 as a world class player, Lasker's other potential challenger was the Polish player, Akiba Rubinstein. In the 1907 tournament at Lodz, **Rubinstein**, as Black, won from the position in diagram 262 in most striking fashion. First came the startling 1 . . . ♖xc3!! allowing white to take the queen by 2 gh (*If 2 ♗xc3 ♗xe4+ 3 ♕xe4 ♕xh2 mate or 2 ♗xb7 ♖xg3 3 ♖f3 ♖xf3 4 ♗xf3 ♘f2+ 5 ♔g1 ♘e4+ 6 ♔f1 ♘d2+ 7 ♔g2 ♗xf3 8 ♕xf3 ♖d2+ wins*) 2 . . . ♖d2!! A further surprising deflection. After 3 ♕xd2 ♗xe4+ 4 ♕g2 ♖h3! and, as mate cannot be put off for more than three moves, White (**Rotlewi**) resigned.

    Rubinstein–Capablanca, played at San Sebastian 1911: 1 d4 d5 2 ♘f3 c5 3 c4 e6 4 cd ed 5 ♘c3 ♘c6 6 g3 ♗e6 (*Nowadays 6 . . . ♘f6 7 ♗g2 ♗e7 8 0–0 0–0 is the accepted order.*) 7 ♗g2 ♗e7 8 0–0 ♖c8 9 dc ♗xc5 10 ♘g5 ♘f6 11 ♘xe6 fe 12 ♗h3 ♕e7 13 ♗g5 0–0 14 ♗xf6 ♕xf6 (*If 14 . . . ♖xf6 15 ♘xd5 ed 16 ♗xc8*) 15 ♘xd5! (diag 263. *On the surface this is a very simple combination — if 15 ed 16 ♕xd5+ ♔h8 17 ♗xc8 wins material; the desperado combination 15 . . . ♗xf2+ 16 ♔g2 ♕h6 17 ♘f4 offers no relief.*

But it's when the side variations are calculated that its profoundness becomes apparent.) 15 . . . ♕h6! (*Now 16 ♘f4 is met by 16 . . . ♖xf4*) 16 ♔g2 ♖cd8! (*Has Rubinstein miscalculated?*) 17 ♕c1!! (*No! It slowly penetrates that this was one of the rare occasions when someone had seen further than the great Cuban. If 17 . . .*

262 B   263 B

♖xd5 18 ♕xh6 gh 19 ♗xe6+.) 17 . . . ed 18 ♕xc5 ♕d2 (*Rubinstein will need to play very well to cash in his extra pawn in the face of the active black pieces.*) 19 ♕b5 ♘d4 20 ♕d3 ♕xd3 21 ed ♖fe8 22 ♗g4! (*22 ♖fe1 ♘c2 23 ♖xe8+ ♖xe8 24 ♖c1 ♘e1+ would give Black counterplay.*) 22 . . . ♖d6! 23 ♖fe1 ♖xe1 24 ♖xe1 ♖b6 25 ♖e5! ♖xb2 26 ♖xd5 ♘c6 27 ♗e6+ ♔f8 28 ♖f5+ ♔e8 29 ♗f7+ ♔d7 30 ♗c4 (*Threatening to force the exchange of rooks by ♖b5.*) 30 . . . a6 31 ♖f7+ ♔d6 32 ♖xg7 b5 33 ♗g8 a5 34 ♖xh7 a4 35 h4 b4 36 ♖h6+ ♔c5 37 ♖h5+ ♔b6 (*If 37 . . . ♔d4 38 ♖d5 leads to the win of the knight.*) 38 ♗d5?! (*A tiny flaw in what otherwise seems a perfectly played game—38 ♗c4 would have been better as White would then have the possibility of ♖b5+ in some variations.*) 38 . . . b3?! (*Rubinstein would have found the game much harder to win after 38 . . . ♖xa2!! as Black can promote after 39 ♗xa2 b3; best would be 39 ♗c4 ♖c2! 40 ♖b5+ ♔c7 41 ♗g8.*) 39 ab! a3 (*If 39 . . . ab 40 ♖h6*) 40 ♗xc6! ♖xb3 (*On 40 . . . a2 White would have 41 ♖b5+ ♔a6 42 ♖b8 a1=♕ 43 ♖h8+ skewering.*) 41 ♗d5 a2 42 ♖h6+! Black resigned. If the king is played to the a-file, White has ♖h8, while 42 . . . ♔b5 also enables White to reach the a-file after 43 ♗c4+. Rubinstein was very proud of this great win.

Alekhine

If Capablanca's contribution to chess was his effortless virtuosity which showed that men may master chess and become unbeatable, and unfortunately, that chess may have become played out, Alekhine's contribution was to demonstrate that where the will existed there was still limitless scope for attack, for complications and for new ideas. The advent of the Soviet School in the thirties served to confirm this viewpoint, and the successes of Bobby Fischer to strengthen this further.

Alexander Alekhine (1892–1946) surprised the chess world when he beat Capablanca in 1927 after a titanic struggle by 6–3, with 25 draws. Capablanca had had his greatest tournament success at New York a few months earlier. Alekhine, an exiled Russian, living in Paris, had achieved the impossible after a super-human exercise in discipline and restraint; he won in his opponent's style.

Examples from Alekhine can be found on pp. 67 and 118. His greatest tournament triumph was at San Remo in 1930 where his score of 13 wins and 2 unwilling draws out-distanced the rest of the field by 3½ points. Alekhine's most satisfying win there must have been the one over his great rival Aron **Nimzowitsch**. Alekhine is White—1 e4 e6 2 d4 d5 3 ♘c3 ♗b4 4 e5 c5 5 ♗d2 ♘e7 5 ♘b5 ♗xd2+ 7 ♕xd2 0–0 8 c3 b6 (*Better 8 . . . ♘f5 followed by . . . ♗d7*) 9 f4 ♗a6 10 ♘f3 ♕d7 11 a4 ♘bc6 12 b4! cb 13 cb ♗b7 14 ♘d6 f5? (*14 . . . a5, to aim for more elbow room, is better.*) 15 a5! ♘c8 16 ♘xb7 ♕xb7 17 a6 ♕f7 18 ♗b5 ♘8e7 19 0–0 h6 20 ♖fc1 ♖ec8 21 ♖c2 ♕e8 22 ♖ac1 (*22 ♖a3! followed by ♖ac3 and ♕c1 is more exact.*) 22 . . . ♖ab8 23 ♕e3 ♖c7 24 ♖c3! ♕d7 25 ♖1c2 ♔f8 26 ♕c1 ♖bc8 27 ♗a4! Black is running out of playable moves. 27 . . . b5 28 ♗xb5 ♔e8 29 ♗a4 ♔d8 30 h4 (diag 264) Black resigned. After 30 . . . ♕e8 31 b5 Black's position collapses.

264
B

Euwe

Holland's Dr Machgielis Euwe (b. 1901) added another shock result when he took Alekhine's world title away from him in 1935 for two years. But it is for his writings, expounding the strategic ideas of the chessboard, that Euwe is best appreciated. **Geller–Euwe**, Zürich 1953, is a fine win, viz. 1 d4 ♘f6 2 c4 e6 3 ♘c3 ♗b4 4 e3 c5 5 a3 ♗xc3+ 6 bc b6 7 ♗d3 ♗b7 8 f3 ♘c6 9 ♘e2 0–0 10 0–0 ♘a5 11 e4 ♘e8 (*In order to contain a white pawn centre after 12 ♗e3 d6 13 ♘g3 ♕d7 14 f4 with 14 . . . f5.*) 12 ♘g3! cd 13 cd ♖c8 (*With pressure on White's c-pawn. If 13 ♕a4 ♗a6 or 13 ♕e2 ♘b3 or 13 ♕c2 ♘xc4 14 ♗xc4 d5.*) 14 f4 ♘xc4 15 f5 (*With the threat of 16 f6 ♘xf6 17 ♗g5 breaking up the pawns around the black king.*) 15 . . . f6 16 ♖f4 b5 (*Another plan is 16 . . . e5 17 ♖h4 ed 18 ♕h5 ♘e5!*)

265
B

17 ♖h4 ♛b6 18 e5! (*Protecting his d-pawn and preparing to open
the diagonal of his bishop at d3.*) 18 ... ♘xe5 19 fe ♘xd3 20 ♛xd3
♛xe6 21 ♛xh7+ ♔f7 22 ♗h6 (diag 265) 22 ... ♖h8! 23 ♛xh8
♖c2 (*The other rook was sacrificed to enable Black to seize the
initiative.*) 24 ♖c1? (*24 d5 would have been somewhat better.*)
24 ... ♖xg2+ 25 ♔f1 ♛b3! (With two mate threats of ... ♛d3+
or ... ♛f3+) 26 ♔e1 ♛f3 White resigned.

Botvinnik and the Soviet School

The greatest of the Soviet world champions is undoubtedly Mikhail
Botvinnik. Following his example there emerged in the USSR a
whole group of world championship class players who were to
dominate the international scene from the 1940s till Fischer broke
through at Reykjavik in 1972. These great masters were Vasily
Smyslov (b. 1921, champion 1957–1958), David Bronstein (b.
1924, tied match 1951). Mikhail Tal (b. 1936, champion 1960–61),
Tigran Petrosian (b. 1929, champion 1963–69) and Boris Spassky
(b. 1937, champion 1969–72).

Botvinnik (b. 1911) clearly won the special world championship
tournament organised in 1948, two years after Alekhine's death. But
his supremacy was beginning to show in the great AVRO tournament in 1938 and was confirmed by the six player Soviet championship event of 1941. Botvinnik's hold on the world title was never
strong; Bronstein and Smyslov drew 24 game matches with him in
1951 and 1954; Smyslov and Tal respectively beat him in 1957 and

1960, but lost return matches in the following year. Here is a Botvinnik game:

Botvinnik–Capablanca, AVRO 1938; **1 d4 ♘f6 2 c4 e6 3 ♘c3 ♗b4 4 e3 d5 5 a3 ♗xc3+ 6 bc c5 7 cd ed 8 ♗d3 0–0 9 ♘e2 b6 10 0–0 ♗a6 11 ♗xa6 ♘xa6 12 ♗b2?!** 12 ♕d3 is better; Black would try to meet this with 12 . . . ♕c8. **12 . . . ♕d7! 13 a4 ♖fe8?** 13 . . . cd 14 cd ♖fc8 would have been stronger. **14 ♕d3 c4** Capablanca decides on the manoeuvre ♘a6–b8–c6–a5–b3 making White's pawn a4 a target. The balance of the game hinges on what play White can create elsewhere. **15 ♕c2 ♘b8 16 ♖ae1 ♘c6** 16 . . . ♘h5, preparing to play 17 . . . f5 and hold back or reduce the effect of White's king-side advance, has been suggested. **17 ♘g3 ♘a5** If 17 . . . ♘e4 **18 ♘h1!** intending to return after 19 f3 **18 f3 ♘b3 19 e4 ♕xa4 20 e5 ♘d7** Now threatening 21 . . . ♘6–b4 **21 ♕f2 g6 22 f4 f5 23 ef ♘xf6 24 f5 ♖xe1 25 ♖xe1 ♖e8 26 ♖e6! ♖xe6 27 fe ♔g7 28 ♕f4!** Intending 29 ♘f5+ gf 30 ♕g5+ **28 . . . ♕e8 29 ♕e5 ♕e7** Or 29 . . . ♘a5 **♗c1!** threatening 31 ♕c7+ followed by ♗h6 or 31 ♗h6+. (diag 266) **30 ♗a3!** Botvinnik has derived his greatest pleasure from the making of this move. **30 . . . ♕xa3** If 30 . . . ♕e8 31 ♕c7+ ♔g8 32 ♗e7 ♘g4 33 ♕d7 wins **31 ♘h5+! gh 32 ♕g5+ ♔f8 33 ♕xf6+ ♔g8 34 e7 ♕c1+ 35 ♔f2 ♕c2+ 36 ♔g3 ♕d3+ 37 ♔h4 ♕e4+ 38 ♔xh5 ♕e2+ 39 ♔h4 ♕e4+ 40 g4 ♕e1+ 41 ♔h5** Black resigned.

Now follows a selection of games played by other leading members of the Soviet school:

Smyslov–Botvinnik, 9th game, match 1954: **1 e4 e6 2 d4 d5 3 ♘c3 ♗b4 4 e5 c5 5 a3 ♗a5!?** (*More usual is 5 . . . ♗xc3+ 6 bc ♘e7.*) **6 b4! cd! 7 ♕g4 ♘e7 8 ba dc 9 ♕xg7 ♖g8 10 ♕xh7 ♘d7 11 ♘f3 ♘f8** (*11 . . . ♕c7!?*) **12 ♕d3 ♕xa5 13 h4 ♗d7 14 ♗g5 ♖c8 15 ♘d4!** (*Smyslov intends to meet 15 . . . ♖c4 with 16 ♕e3 ♖a4 17 ♖b1 ♗xa3 18 ♘b5! with multi-threats.*) **15 . . . ♘f5 16 ♖b1!** (*This parries 16 . . . ♘xd4 17 ♕xd4 ♗b5.*) **16 . . . ♖c4 17 ♘xf5 ef 18 ♖xb7 ♖e4+?!** (diag 267) **19 ♕xe4! de 20 ♖b8+ ♗c8 21 ♗b5+**

266
W

267
W

♛xb5   22 ♖xb5 ♘e6   23 ♗f6 ♖xg2   24 h5 ♗a6   25 h6 Black resigned.

Pachman–Bronstein, Prague–Moscow 1946: 1 d4 ♘f6   2 c4 d6   3 ♘c3 e5   4 ♘f3 ♘bd7   5 g3 g6   6 ♗g2 ♗g7   7 0–0 0–0   8 b3 ♖e8   9 e4 ed   10 ♘xd4 ♘c5   11 ♖e1 a5   12 ♗b2 a4   13 ♖ac1 (*If 13 b4 a3!*) 13 . . . c6   14 ♗a1 ab   15 ab ♛b6   16 h3 ♘fd7 (*Intending . . . ♘f8–e6 with increased pressure against b3*) 17 ♖b1 ♘f8   18 ♔h2 (*Preparing f2–f4*) 18 . . . h5   19 ♖e2 (*If 19 f4 h4   20 g4 ♘fe6*) 19 . . . h4   20 ♖d2 (diag 268) 20 . . . ♖xa1!! (*Initiating a fantastic combination involving complex operations over the whole board.*) 21 ♖xa1 ♗xd4   22 ♖xd4 ♘xb3   23 ♖xd6 ♛xf2!! (*Bronstein advanced the pawn to h4 on move 19 in order now to answer 24 ♛xb3 with 24 . . . hg+   25 ♔h1 ♗xh3!   26 ♖g1 ♗xg2+   27 ♖xg2 ♛f1+   28 ♖g1 ♛h3 mate.*) 24 ♖a2 ♛xg3+   25 ♔h1 ♛xc3   26 ♖a3 (*If 26 ♖d3 ♛c1!*) 26 . . . ♗xh3   27 ♖xb3 ♗xg2+   28 ♔xg2 ♛xc4   29 ♖d8 ♛e6   30 ♖xb7 ♖a8   31 ♛e2 h3+ White resigned. This game helped considerably to popularise the defence used, the King's Indian.

Tal's play as a boy is depicted on p. 72. Here is **Tal–Suetin**, Tbilisi 1969–70: 1 e4 c5   2 ♘f3 e6   3 d4 cd   4 ♘xd4 a6   5 ♗d3

♘e7 (*5 . . . ♘f6!*) 6 ♘c3 ♘bc6 7 ♘b3 ♘g6 8 0–0 b5 9 ♗e3 d6 10 f4 ♗e7 11 ♕h5! (*If now Black goes 11 . . . 0–0 White has ♖f1–f3– h3.*) 11 . . . ♗f6 12 ♖ad1! ♗xc3?! (*Preferable is 12 . . . ♕c7.*) 13 bc ♕c7 14 ♖d2 ♘e7 (*Suetin hopes that his own position is safe and sound and that he can exploit the weakness of White's double c-pawns. Tal looks for a point of entry in Suetin's position.*) 15 ♘d4! ♗d7 16 f5! ef 17 ef ♘e5 18 ♘e6! ♗xe6 19 fe g6 (diag 269. *On hindsight 19 . . . 0–0–0 would have been safer.*) 20 ♕xe5! de 21 ef+ Black resigned. 21 . . . ♔f8 would allow 22 ♗h6 mate while after 21 . . . ♔d7 22 ♗f5++ ♔c6 23 ♗e4+ would be murder.

Petrosian–Portisch, 13th game, match 1974: 1 ♘f3 d5 2 d4 e6 3 c4 ♘f6 4 ♗g5 ♗e7 5 ♘c3 0–0 6 ♖c1 h6 7 ♗h4 b6 8 cd ♘xd5 9 ♘xd5 ed 10 ♗xe7 ♕xe7 11 g3 ♗a6 (*Uhlmann–Veresov, East Germany–Byelorussia 1971, went 11 . . . ♖e8 12 ♗g2 ♗a6 13 ♘e5 ♘d7 14 ♖xc7 ♖ac8!?*) 12 e3 c5 13 ♗xa6 ♘xa6 14 0–0 ♘c7 (*If 14 . . . c4 Petrosian intended 15 b3.*) 15 b3 ♖ac8 16 ♖e1 ♖fd8 17 h4 (*Against Black's manoeuvre ♘c7–e6–g5*) 17 . . . ♘e6 (*Possibility 17 . . . ♘e8 to be followed by . . . ♘f5 is better.*) 18 ♕d3 ♕f6 19 ♔g2 cd 20 ed (*White could also retain some advantage by 20 ♖xc8 ♖xc8 21 ed to be followed by ♖e5 or ♕a6.*) 20 . . . ♖xc1 21 ♖xc1 ♕f4!? (*The queen is en route to either g4 or e4.*) 22 gf!! (A remarkable approach to the position. In return for the pawn

269
W.

sacrificed White's pieces become active and the black knight is relegated to a series of out-of-the-way squares.) 22 . . . ♘xf4+ 23 ♔g3 ♘xd3 24 ♖c3 ♘b4 (*The improbable 24 . . . ♘b2! 25 ♖c2 ♘d3 is a possibility.*) 25 a3 ♘a6 26 b4 (diag 270. *According to Petrosian Black could now try to hold his position with 26 . . . ♖d7.*) 26 . . . ♘b8 27 ♖c7 a5 (*If 27 . . . a6 28 ♘e5 f6 29 ♘g6 leaves Black hard pressed.*) 28 b5! ♘d7 29 ♔f4 (*All the white pieces have potentially active roles.*) 29 . . . h5 (*Or 29 . . . ♘f8 30 ♖b7 ♖d6 31 ♘e5 ♘g6 32 ♘xg6 fg 33 ♔e5*) 30 ♘e5 ♘f8 31 ♖b7 f6 32 ♘c6 ♘g6+ 33 ♔g3 ♖d6! 34 ♖xb6 ♖e6 35 ♖b8+ ♘f8 (*If 35 . . .*

270
B

♔h7 38 ♖d8) 36 ♖a8 ♖e1 37 ♘d8 (*37 b6 ♖b1 38 ♘b4 also wins.*) 37 . . . ♔h7 38 b6 ♖b1 39 b7 ♘d7 40 ♖xa5 Black resigned.

For the Spassky–Rashkovsky game, with Spassky playing in his best style, turn to p. 73.

Fischer

Robert J. Fischer (USA, b. 9 March 1943) by beating Boris Spassky in 1972, became the first non-Soviet player to win the title since

1948. There follows three of his games:

Robert Byrne-Fischer, USA Championship Dec. 1963: 1 d4 ♘f6 2 c4 g6 3 g3 c6 4 ♗g2 d5 5 cd cd 6 ♘c3 ♗g7 7 e3 0–0 8 ♘ge2 ♘c6 9 0–0 b6 10 b3 ♗a6 11 ♗a3 ♖e8! 12 ♕d2 e5! 13 de ♘xe5 14 ♖fd1 (*As analysis after the game showed, this was the wrong rook. On 14 ♖ad1 Fischer suggested 14 . . . ♕c8 with about even chances.*) 14 . . . ♘d3! 15 ♕c2 ♘xf2!! 16 ♔xf2 ♘g4+ 17 ♔g1 ♘xe3 18 ♕d2 ♘xg2!! 19 ♔xg2 d4 20 ♘xd4 ♗b7+ 21 ♔f1 (*diag 272. If 21 ♔f2 Black can play for mate by 21 . . . ♕d7 22 ♖ac1 ♕h3 23 ♘f3 ♗h6 24 ♕d3 ♗e3+. On 21 ♔g1 Black has 21 . . . ♗xd4+ 22 ♕xd4 ♖e1+ 23 ♔f2 ♕xd4 24 ♖xd4 ♖xa1.*) 21 . . . ♕d7!! and while the spectators in a side room were debating how Byrne would win, the news reached them that Byrne had resigned! He saw that if 22 ♕f2 ♕h3+ 23 ♔g1, the deflecting 23 . . . ♖e1+ (and he was sure Fischer would see it) 24 ♖xe1 ♗xd4 would force mate.

Tringov–Fischer, Havana 1965, with Fischer playing by Telex from New York: 1 e4 c5 2 ♘f3 d6 3 d4 cd 4 ♘xd4 ♘f6 5 ♘c3 a6 6 ♗g5 e6 7 f4 ♛b6 8 ♛d2 ♛xb2 9 ♖b1 ♛a3 10 e5 de 11 fe ♘fd7 12 ♗c4 ♗b4 13 ♖b3 ♛a5 14 0–0 0–0 15 ♘xe6!? fe 16 ♗xe6+ ♔h8 17 ♖xf8+ ♗xf8 18 ♛f4 (diag 273) 18 . . . ♘c6! 19 ♛f7 ♛c5+ 20 ♔h1 ♘f6! 21 ♗xc8 (*If 21 ef ♗xe6 22 fg+ ♗xg7 23 ♛xe6 ♛xg5 or 21 ♗xf6 ♗xe6 22 ♛xe6 gf 23 ♛xf6+ ♗g7 and Black would win in both cases.*) 21 . . . ♘xe5 22 ♛e6 ♘5g4 and White resigned. This is typical of the complicated lines that Fischer, when Black, is willing to play and which he backs with painstaking study at home beforehand.

Fischer–Petrosian, 7th game, match 1971: 1 e4 c5 2 ♘f3 e6 3 d4 cd 4 ♘xd4 a6 5 ♗d3 ♘c6 6 ♘xc6 bc 7 0–0 d5 8 c4 ♘f6 9 cd cd 10 ed ed 11 ♘c3 ♗e7 12 ♛a4+! (diag 274) Fischer, in his games, shows a marked trait to disrupt the even flow of an opponent's mobilisation. This intends, after 12 . . . ♗d7 13 ♛c2! 0–0 to put Black's pawns under pressure with 14 ♗g5. 12 . . . ♛d7!? 13 ♖e1! This is much superior to winning the exchange—bishop for rook—by 13 ♗b5. 13 . . . ♛xa4 14 ♘xa4 ♗e6 15 ♗e3 0–0 16 ♗c5! In order to remove Black's potentially most active bishop. 16 . . . ♖fe8 Livelier is 16 . . . ♗xc5 17 ♘xc5 ♖fb8! 17 ♗xe7 ♖xe7 18 b4! This keeps Black's a-pawn fixed for target practice. 18 . . .

273
B

274
B

♔f8 19 ♘c5 ♗c8 20 f3 ♖ea7 21 ♖e5 ♗d7! 22 ♘xd7+! ♖xd7 23 ♖c1 24 ♖c6 is the threat. 23 . . . ♖d6 24 ♖c7 ♘d7 25 ♖e2 Black is tied up; if his knight moves White has ♖2e7. 25 . . . g6 26 ♔f2 h5 27 f4 h4? 28 ♔f3 f5 29 ♔e3 d4+ 30 ♔d2 ♘b6 31 ♖2e7 ♘d5 32 ♖f7+ ♔e8 33 ♖b7 ♘xb4 34 ♗c4 Black resigned. The threat is 35 ♖h7 ♖f6 36 ♖h8+ ♖f8 37 ♗f7+ ♔d8 38 ♖xf8 mate. The clarity of Fischer's positional play as White is in contrast to his approach when Black in the Tringov game.

Karpov

The hallmark of Karpov's games is fluency and ease. He is the Mozart of the chessboard and in chess terms he enjoys Capablanca's speed of play, the invincibility of Petrosian in his best days and the killer instinct of Fischer.

Anatoly Karpov (b. 23.5.1951) became World Champion in 1975 when Fischer refused to defend his title. He has successfully defended his title twice by 6–5 with 21 draws against Korchnoi in Baguio City 1978 and by 6–2 with 10 draws in Merano 1981.

He is one of the most successful tournament players ever, winning several of the top events each year. The following game helped him to first prize at the 'super tournament' in Tilburg 1983.

Karpov–Seirawan, Tilburg 1983. 1 e4 c6 2 d4 d5 3 ♘d2 de
4 ♘xe4 ♗f5 5 ♘g3 ♗g6 6 h4 h6 7 ♘f3 ♘d7 8 h5 ♗h7 9 ♗d3
♗xd3 10 ♕xd3 ♕c7 11 ♗d2 ♘gf6 12 0–0–0 e6 13 ♘e4 ♗d6!?
(*An interesting new move; previously 13 . . . 0–0–0 and 13 . . . ♗e7
had been preferred.*) 14 ♘xd6+ ♕xd6 15 ♕e2 ♕d5 16 ♔b1!? ♘xh5
17 ♘e5 ♘hf6 18 f3 b5 (*After 18 . . . ♕xd4 19 ♗c3 ♕c5 20 ♗d4
♕e7 21 ♘xd7 ♘xd7 22 ♗xg7 ♖g8 23 ♗d4, White stands slightly
better.*) 19 g4 ♖g8 20 ♖he1 ♘b6 (diag 275; *20 . . . ♕xd4? 21
♘xf7 winning*) 21 b3!! (*21 f4 ♘fd7 22 f5 ♘xe5 23 de ♕c4 followed by . . . 0–0–0 is satisfactory for Black*) 21 . . . ♕d6 22 f4
♘fd7 23 f5 ♘xe5 24 de ♕c5 25 fe fe 26 ♗e3! ♕xe5 (*26 . . . ♕c3
is met by 27 ♖d6!*) 27 ♗xb6 ♕xe2 28 ♖xe2 ab 29 ♖xe6+ ♔f7
30 ♖xc6 ♖gd8 31 ♖f1+ ♔g8 32 ♖f5! (*Accurate to the end; if 32
♖xb6 ♖d5 33 ♖f5 ♖xf5 34 gf ♔f7 when White still has work to
do.*) 32 . . . ♖d1+ 33 ♔b2 ♖g1 34 ♖xb5 ♖xg4 35 ♖cxb6 g6 36
♖b8+ ♖xb8 37 ♖xb8+ ♔g7 38 a4 ♖e4 39 a5 ♖e7 40 a6 ♔f6
41 b4 g5 42 b5 ♖a7 43 ♖b6+ Black resigns.

275
W

Korchnoi

Viktor Korchnoi has been continuously involved in the Candidates'
stage of the World Championship cycle since 1968, and from 1974
until 1981 he was Karpov's sole antagonist in the three matches
which decided the destination of the world title itself.

Korchnoi's record of achievement and experience is formidable.
Indeed, after 31 games at Baguio 1978 he was within one win of
the supreme title.

At the age of 52 he is still producing vintage performances as in
the following win over many times Candidate Lajos Portisch. (Notes
by Raymond Keene)

Korchnoi–Portisch, Candidates match, game 3, 1983. 1 c4 c5
2 ♘f3 ♘c6 3 ♘c3 ♘f6 4 d4 cd 5 ♘xd4 e6 6 ♘db5 (*At this point
Korchnoi used to favour 6 g3. The move played leads by force to
early simplification, but Korchnoi has never been one to back away*

from the endgame.) 6 . . . d5 7 ♗f4 e5 8 cd ef 9 dc bc 10 ♕xd8+ ♚xd8 11 ♘d4 (*A refined new idea. Normally White seeks to gain a development tempo with 11 ♖d1+ or 11 0–0–0+ but Korchnoi has seen that it can be of equal importance to gain time by immediately threatening the pawn on c6.)* 11 . . . ♚c7 12 g3 ♗c5?! (*Asking for trouble on the c-file. Best is 12 . . . ♗b4 followed by . . . ♗xc3.*)

13 ♖c1! fg 14 hg ♗a6 (*The last chance is 14 . . . ♖b8! 15 ♘b3 ♗b4 16 ♗g2 ♗e6.*) 12 ♘xc6! (diag 276) 15 . . . ♗b7 16 ♘a4! (*Accurate. Not 16 ♗g2? ♗xc6 17 ♗xc6 ♗xf2+ 18 ♔xf2 ♘g4+.*) 16 . . . ♗xf2+ 17 ♔xf2 ♘e4+ 18 ♔g1 ♗xc6 19 ♗g2 ♖ae8 20 ♖h4 f5 21 g4 f4 22 ♖xc6+! (*The final blow which completes the undermining of Black's structure and reaps a decisive material advantage.*) 22 . . . ♔xc6 23 ♘c3 ♔c5 24 ♗xe4 ♔d4 25 ♗f3 ♖b8 26 ♘a4 ♖b4 27 ♖h5 ♖d8 28 b3 h6 29 ♔f2 ♖d6 30 ♖f5 g5 31 ♖f7 ♔e5 32 ♖xa7 ♖d2 33 ♘c5 ♖bd4 34 ♖a6 ♖d6 35 ♖a5 Black resigns.

Kasparov

The direct style and youthful optimism of the young man from Baku has captured the imagination of the chess public in the 1980s. Like Alekhine and Fischer he is not content to play colourless draws and yet he has recently produced technical masterpieces which demonstrate his all-round virtuosity.

Gary Kasparov (b. 1963) became a Grandmaster in 1980 and won the Soviet Championship in 1981. Victories over Belyavsky (6-3), Korchnoi (7-4) and Smyslov (8½-4½) gave him the chance to challenge Karpov in September 1984.

One of the most decisive games of his match against Korchnoi was the following game: (Notes from *Informator* 36)

Kasparov-Korchnoi, Candidates' Match, game 7, 1983. 1 d4 ♘f6 2 c4 e6 3 g3 d5 4 ♗g2 dc 5 ♘f3 ♗d7!? (*According to all published annals, this is a new move, but Najdorf claims that he played it 50 years ago!*) 6 ♕c2 (*If 6 ♘e5 ♗c6!*) 6 . . . c5 7 0–0 ♗c6 8 ♕xc4 ♘bd7 9 ♗g5 ♖c8 10 ♗xf6 ♘xf6 (*Or 10 . . . ♕xf6 11 ♘c3 threatening d5.*) 11 dc ♗xf3 12 ♗xf3 ♗xc5 (*With the tactical threat of . . . ♗xf2+ and . . . ♖xc4. Black has liquidated the central pawns and achieved near parity in development and the only problem he faces is the slight weakness of his b7 pawn.*) 13 ♕b5+ ♕d7 14 ♘c3 ♕xb5 15 ♘xb5 ♔e7 16 b4! (diag 277. *Without this excellent move White would have nothing; 16 ♗xb7 ♖b8 only gets White's minor pieces*

276
B

277
B

into a hopeless tangle.) 16 . . . ♗xb4 17 ♘xa7 ♖c7? (*After this careless error Black is lost, since he cannot defend his exposed b7 pawn. The only resistance lies in 17 . . . ♖a8 19 ♘b5 ♖fb8 20 ♖fc1 ♘e8!*) 18 ♖fc1 ♖d7 19 ♖ab1 ♗d2 (*Now if 19 . . . ♖a8? just 20 ♘c8+ wins.*) 20 ♖c2 ♖hd8 21 ♗xb7 ♔f8 22 ♘c6 ♖c7 23 ♖bb2 ♖d6! 24 a4 ♗e1 25 ♖b1! (*After 25 a5, Black obtains counterplay with 25 . . . ♘g4! 26 f3 ♘e3 27 a6?! ♖d1!*) 25 . . . ♘d5 26 ♗a8 ♖c8 27 ♗b7 ♖c7 28 ♖c4! ♘e7 29 ♘e5 ♗a5 30 ♖b5 ♘g6 31 ♘c6 (*After this Black can resign without qualms. There is a truly aesthetic quality to White's concentration of forces on the queenside light squares.*) 31 . . . ♖d1+ 32 ♔g2 ♗e1 33 a5 ♘e7 34 a6 ♘xc6 35 ♖xc6 ♖xc6 36 ♗xc6 ♖a1 37 ♖b8+ ♔e7 38 ♖b7+ ♔d6 39 ♗b5 ♗c3 40 ♖xf7 ♗f6 41 ♖d7+ ♔c5 42 ♗d3 h6 43 ♖b7 ♖a3 44 a7 ♔d5 45 f3 ♔d6 46 ♖b6+ Black resigned. *Notes by Raymond Keene.*

Adams

Edward Adams is known in chess circles only for his play in one game. Played in New Orleans in 1920, that game has become one of the classics of chess! Adams had White against the Mexican Master, Carlos Torre, then sixteen years old. The opening is colourless, but the end of the game is distinguished by the perfect exploitation of Black's back rank weakness.

The game began **1 e2—e4 e7—e5 2 ♘g1—f3 d7—d6** This is known as Philidor's Defence. It's not particularly popular, no doubt due to the self-imposed limiting of the bishop at f8. **3 d2—d4** This open up more lines for the white pieces and threatens to win a pawn by 4 d4xe5 d6xe5 5 ♕xd8+ ♔xd8 6 ♘xe5! **3 . . . e5xd4** This is unusual, but it has been played in recent years by the famous Danish grandmaster, Bent Larsen. **4 ♕d1xd4** Taking with the knight is equally playable; in reply Black would play 4 . . . g6, intending to 'fianchetto' his f8 bishop at g7. **4 . . . ♘b8—c6** Attacking White's queen; the reply, **5 ♗f1—b5**, pins the knight to the diagonal of the black king. **5 . . . ♗c8—d7** Unpinning and renewing the attack on White's queen. **6 ♗b5xc6 ♗d7xc6** The white queen has an untroubled, dominant position (diag 278). **7 ♘b1—c3 ♘g8—f6** Both players develop either pieces. **8 0—0** Maybe better is 8 ♗g5, followed

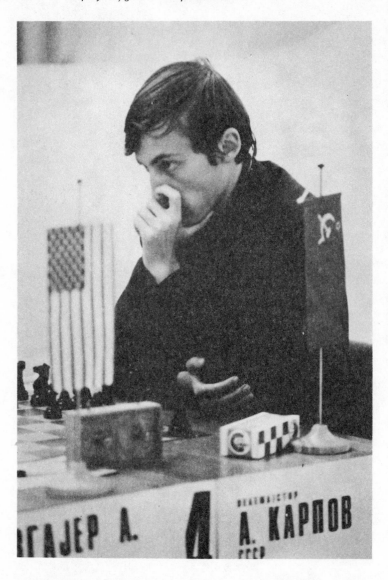

by 0—0—0 and then, either ♖he1 or some advance of the f, g and h pawns if Black should castle on that wing. **8 . . . ♗f8—e7 9 ♘c3—d5** This post is sometimes ideal for a knight, but here it is quickly swapped off without White gaining any advantage; however, Black can't afford 9 . . . ♘xd5 as 10 ed hits Black's bishop and leaves his position in a tangle, e.g. on 10 . . . ♗f6 White can win a piece by

11 ♕e4+. **9 . . . ♘c6xd5** If this exchange is delayed—say Black castles instead—White supports the knight with his c-pawn and gains more space for manoeuvring. **10 e4xd5 0—0 11 ♗c1-g5** (diag 279) **11 . . . c7—c6** 11 . . . ♘xd5 is answered simply by 12 ♕xd5, adding to the protection of the bishop. But Black could prepare such a combination; it would work after 11 . . . h6! 12 ♗h4 ♘xd5 13 ♕xd5 ♗xh4 14 ♘xh4 ♕xh4 15 ♕xb7 ♕c4 when Black has no difficulties. The additional advantage of the pawn move 11 . . . h6 is that Black's king has an escape square from the back row, the lack of which he will regret.

278
W

279
B

12 c2—c4 c6xd5 13 c4xd5 ♖f8—e8 14 ♖f1—e1 a7—a5 15 ♖e1—e2 White is starting to double the rooks. **15 . . . ♖a8—c8** Torre, not fully alert to the critical nature of his problems along the e-file, continues formal development. Instead 15 . . . ♘d7! would have been better; then if White doubles by 16 ♖ae1 Black can go 16 . . . f6 followed by 17 . . . ♘e5.

After the move played, White produces a series of dazzling moves, as well-conceived and relevant as the finest play of the greatest masters. **16 ♖a1—e1.** With this doubling of the rooks, White threatens 17 ♗xf6; then recapture by the bishop would cost Black his queen for a rook, viz. 17 . . . ♗xf6 18 ♖xe8+ ♕xe8 19 ♖xe8+; the pawn recapture weakens Black's king's position. **16 . . . ♕d8—d7 17 ♗g5xf6** (diag 280) **17 . . . ♗e7xf6**

17 . . . g7xf6 would have been comparatively better. It sets a subtle trap; if then White plays 18 ♖xe7 hoping for 18 . . . ♖xe7 19 ♖xe7 ♕xe7 20 ♕g4 forking king and rook. Black would play 18 . . . ♕xe7!! as White's own back row would be inadequately guarded—19 ♖xe7 ♖c1+.

In the game again, with White to move. At the moment Black needs both his rook at c8 and queen at d7 to protect his rook at e8 against capture and mate. Therefore both guardians have limited scope in other directions.

18 ♕d4–g4!! Black's queen is attacked and it must stay on the a4–d7 diagonal to protect the e8 rook. **18 . . . ♕d7–b5** A curious situation: Black threatens 19 . . . ♕xe2 and if White recaptures by 20 ♖xe2 Black mates 20 . . . ♖c1–21 ♖e1 ♖xe1+ 22 ♘xe1 ♖xe1. **19 ♕g4–c4!!** This shuts out Black's idea, and bears on both of the e8-rook's defenders. **19 . . . ♕b5–d7 20 ♕c4–c7!** It's the same story—White's queen cannot be taken, and Black's queen must be found a safe square along the e8–a4 diagonal. **20 . . . ♕d7–b5** If 20 . . . ♕a4 White wins by 21 ♖e4! as this rook move involves the desperado combination 21 . . . ♖f8 22 ♕xc8 ♕xe4 23 ♕xf8+ winning a rook. White also must be careful; the 'brilliant' 21 ♕xb7?! would have come to grief against Black's 21 . . . ♕xe2 22 ♕xc8 ♕xe1+.

The game continued **21 a2–a4** (diag 281) **21 . . . ♕b5xa4** (Two other variations must be calculated:—if 21 . . . ♖xe2 then 22 ♕xc8+ or 21 . . . ♕xe2 when 22 ♖xe2 leaves Black helpless.)

Play went **22 ♖e2–e4 ♕a4-b5.** Black could have tried two other ideas:
1) 22 . . . h6 23 ♕xc8 ♕xe4 24 ♕xe8+ which loses him a rook, and
2) 22 . . . ♔f8 23 ♕xd6+ ♗e7 24 ♖xe7 with White winning at least a bishop. Black has no defence.

The game finished with **23 ♕c7xb7.** This is now possible with white's rook on e4 instead of at e2. Black cannot save both his king and queen, and so he resigned the game. Wonderful play by Edward Adams!

Chess Computers

People have always been fascinated by the idea of a machine that could play chess, and it is not really surprising that in 1770 a young Austrian engineer named Wolfgang Kempelen constructed an ingenious machine that won nearly every game it ever played. This machine, 'The Turk', defeated Napoleon in 1809 and subsequent imitations also performed famous feats and made money for their inventors. These 'machines' were all frauds, of course,—inside each, a small but strong human chess master was cunningly concealed!

True computer chess dates from 1950, not long after the first electronic 'brains' were invented. An American, Claude Shannon, developed in 1950 the first chess-playing programme which, though very humble, could defeat untutored human players. Shannon's programme involved translating the values (material and positional) of the chess-board into numbers, and on this basis a lot of work has been done in the last 25 years—especially in the USA, and in the USSR, where ex-world champion Mikhail Botvinnik, has been a moving force.

Botvinnik's claim that there will be, before long, computer masters and grandmasters, is not, however, taken seriously by many informed people. The difficulty seems to lie as much with the human programmers, who cannot express mathematically the intuitive processes of a master, as with the technical capacity of the machines.

There are still many problems to be ironed out of computer programs, one of the most well-known being the 'horizon effect.' David Levy describes this in the *Chess Computer Handbook*—in the following position (diag 282) it is Black to move, and although White is a long way behind in material, Black must cede most of the extra material because of what is happening on the a1–h8 diagonal. Thus a program which looks ahead 2-ply (one move for each side) will play . . . ᐁb2 or . . . ᐁc3 because that move only loses a knight, whereas alternatives lose a queen for a bishop! What the program has done is push the loss of the queen for a bishop over its horizon, so that it can longer see the loss as being inevitable.

However, chess computers are making progress. In 1983 a computer demonstrated a win in the ending of king and two bishops against king and knight which had been thought drawn for half a century and there is a 'database' which plays the ending king and queen against king and rook perfectly.

In the 3rd Commonwealth championship in Hong Kong 1984, the Novag Constellation scored 4/11 achieving a rating of approximately 2120 ELO (190 BCF) the highest to date for a commercially available microcomputer.

This was one of its games against a player rated 2260.

Constellation–K. Schepel, Commonwealth Championship, Hong Kong 1984. 1 e4 e5 2 ᐁf3 ᐁc6 3 ♗b5 ᐁge7 4 0–0 g6 5 c3 ♗g7 6 d4 a6 7 ♗xc6 ᐁxc6 8 de ᐁxe5 9 ᐁxe5 ♗xe5 10 f4 ♗g7 11 f5 f6 12 fg hg 13 ♗e3 d6 14 ᐁd2 ♕e7 15 ♕b3 f5 16 ♖ae1 ♗e5 17 ♗f4 ♗xf4 18 ♖xf4 g5 19 ᐁf3 gf 20 ef ♕xe1+ 21 ᐁxe1 ♗xf5 22 ♕xb7 ♔d7 23 ♕b4 ♖he8 24 ᐁf3 ♗e4 25 ♕a4+ c6 26 ♔f2 a5 (diag 283) 27 ♕d4 c5 28 ♕c4 ♖ab8 29 b3 ♚c6 30 ♘g5 d5 31 ♕a6+ ♚d7 32 ♕xa5 ♖a8 33 ♕b5+ ♚e7 32 ♕xc5+ ♚f6 35 ♘xe4 de 36 ♕d4+ ♚f5 37 ♕d7+ ♚f6 38 ♕d6+ ♚g5 39 a4 ♖ad8 40 ♕c7 e3+ 41 ♚f3 e2 42 ♕g7+ ♚f5 43 ♕f7+ ♚g5 44 ♕xf4+ ♚g6 45 ♕g4+ ♚f6 46 ♕h4+ ♚f7 47 ♕h5+ ♚f6 (½–½)

Additional features of chess microcomputers are being developed all the time. Sensor boards and LCD displays are now common, while machines with magnets which move the pieces for the computer have now appeared. A model with a robotic arm is also on the market.

How strong can computers become? David Levy believes that between the years 1995 and 2000, a computer will play at the level of a strong Grandmaster under tournament conditions while at blitz play the strongest computers have already claimed a number of Grandmaster scalps.

Chess Problems

The art of composing and solving set move positions, White to play and mate in x (usually 2 or 3) moves, is an interesting world of its own, having only minimum relations with the hurly-burly of the players' cut-throat world. These compositions are puzzles and yet they have more. One can admire their settings; and the way that ideas are blended and expressed within them. They are expected to conform to certain standards; there must be a use for every piece on the board; alternative solutions (cooks) are normally unacceptable; a key move giving check is grudgingly accepted only when the idea outweighs its execution.

The first position given (diag 284) was constructed by a famous 9th century composer, Abu'n Na'am, who was probably under the patronage of the Caliphs of Baghdad. Black is to move and win (actually to mate on his third move). The solution runs 1 ... ♘h4+ 2 ♖xh4 ♖xg3+ 3 ♚xg3 ♖e3 mate. It was characteristic of problems of that era for the losing side to be on the verge of an overwhelming

Black to play and win | White to play and mate in 2

win. Possibly money was wagered on the outcome of the position with the odds apparently stacked heavily in favour of the losing side.

There are four grandmasters for chess compositions recognised (in early 1974) by the Federation International des Echecs (FIDE). These include Comins Mansfield of England, who was born in 1896. Diagram 285, was published by *The Morning Post* (now incorporated with *The Daily Telegraph*) in 1923. White is to play and mate in two. If Black was to play, White would have no difficulties—1 ... d3 2 ♕e7; 1 ... ♖g1 (or 3–8) 2 ♘1e2; 1 ... ♖h (or a–f) 2 2 ♘g3. But White has no good waiting move, his king moves allowing Black to check. In search for the solution one is tempted to look for knight mates in similar fashion, but it is the queen that mates after 1 ♕a6— threatening mates at e2 or g6 according to which way the black rook jumps; if 1 ... d3 2 ♕e6 mate.

Answers to self-assessments (p. 100–101)

Discussing your first reactions: they could be: 1 ... ♖b8—saving the rook; 1 ... ♗g4—counter-attacking on to White's queen; 1 ... ♗g4 intending 2 ... ♕d3 and 3 ... ♕e2 mate—attacking; 1 ... ♕d3 intending 2 ... ♗g4 and 3 ... ♕e2 mate—attacking; 1 ... ♕e7—very wild; 1 ... ♘xe4 to approach the White king by ... ♕h4+ and/or ... ♗f2+ attacking; 1 ... ♗a6 intending 2 ... ♕d3—attacking.

Deep consideration could lead to one switching through all these possibilities. That would mean you have a wide ranging balanced approach to positions.

When calculated out Black's best is 1 ... ♘xe4 and if 2 ♗xa8 ♗f2+ 3 ♔e2 ♗g4+ wins the white queen, or 2 ♗xe4 ♕h4+ and 3 ... ♕xe4, or 2 d4! ♕f6 3 ♗xe4 ♕h4+ 4 ♔d2 ♕xe4 with the white king a long-term target.

Descriptive Notation

In descriptive notation, squares are named according to the number of the square along the file of the initial placing of the pieces, in abbreviated form. The squares are named from both the black and white side of the board, which means that each square has two names.

The initial square of White's queen is Queen 1 (abbreviated to Q1). Squares along the file from Q1 read Q2, Q3 . . . to Q8. The squares on the king file are described as K1, K2 . . . The black king, from White's point of view starts at K8, and from Black's point of view on K1.

The rook on the queen's side is regarded as the queen's rook (QR) and squares are labelled QR1, QR2. . . . The queen's knight

White

	h	g	f	e	d	c	b	a	
1	KR1	KN1	KB1	K1	Q1	QB1	QN1	QR1	1
	KR8	KN8	KB8	K8	Q8	QB8	QN8	QR8	
2	KR2	KN2	KB2	K2	Q2	QB2	QN2	QR2	2
	KR7	KN7	KB7	K7	Q7	QB7	QN7	QR7	
3	KR3	KN3	KB3	K3	Q3	QB3	QN3	QR3	3
	KR6	KN6	KB6	K6	Q6	QB6	QN6	QR6	
4	KR4	KN4	KB4	K4	Q4	QB4	QN4	QR4	4
	KR5	KN5	KB5	K5	Q5	QB5	QN5	QR5	
5	KR5	KN5	KB5	K5	Q5	QB5	QN5	QR5	5
	KR4	KN4	KB4	K4	Q4	QB4	QN4	QR4	
6	KR6	KN6	KB6	K6	Q6	QB6	QN6	QR6	6
	KR3	KN3	KB3	K3	Q3	QB3	QN3	QR3	
7	KR7	KN7	KB7	K7	Q7	QB7	QN7	QR7	7
	KR2	KN2	KB2	K2	Q2	QB2	QN2	QR2	
8	KR8	KN8	KB8	K8	Q8	QB8	QN8	QR8	8
	KR1	KN1	KB1	K1	Q1	QB1	QN1	QR1	
	h	g	f	e	d	c	b	a	

Black

(QN) and queen's bishop (QB) are treated similarly. The king-side pieces are prefixed by the letter K, e.g. KR, KN and KB.

The prefixes K and Q are dropped when there is no ambiguity, e.g. when the bishop on KB1 goes to QB4 (B—QB4) it can be written as B—B4 if the other bishop cannot go to KB4.

Captures are indicated by x, e.g. BxN means bishop takes knight.

Other moves have a dash in the middle in place of 'to', e.g. P—K4 being pawn to king's fourth.

When it's necessary to distinguish between pieces in greater detail, one adds square on which the piece is, or will be placed, e.g. N/K5xN/N6.

Descriptive notation is slowly becoming unfashionable. It is more cumbersome to use than the algebriac notation used throughout most of this book.

An example of a game in descriptive notation is the following great win by Paul Keres of Estonia, a leading player for many years:

Keres-Panno, Gothenburg 1955: **1 P—K4 P—QB4 2 N—KB3 P—Q3 3 P—Q4 PxP 4 NxP N—KB3 5 N—QB3 P—QR3 6 B—KN5 P—K3 7 P—B4 Q—N3 8 Q—Q2!** At the time of this game an original idea. With it Spassky scored one of his two actual wins over Fischer at Reykjavik. **8 . . . N—B3** Fischer played 8 . . . QxNP. **9 0—0—0 QxN 10 QxQ NxQ 11 RxN N—Q2** If 11 . . . B—K2 12 B—K2 followed by KR—Q1 would give White a strong positional grip. **12 B—K2 P—R3 13 B—R4 P—KN4 14 PxP N—K4** On 14 . . . B—K2 White plays 15 B—N3. **15 N—R4! B—K2** White, after 15 . . . P—N4 16 N—N6 R—QN1 17 NxB RxN, can undermine Black's queen-side with 18 P—R4. **16 N—N6 R—QN1 17 B—N3 PxP 18 R/R1—Q1** (diag 271) White threatens 19 BxN PxB 20 R—B4. **18 . . . P—B3 19 P—B4 21 P—B5 P—B5 22 PxP BxP 23 RxB PxB 24 PxP R—B2?!** *With 24 . . . K—B2! Black would show more fight.* **25 K—N1 R—B2 26 R—Q8+ K—N2 27 R—QB1! N—B3 28 P—K5 K—N3 29 B—Q3+ K—B2** *Or 29 . . . K—R4 30 R—R8+ K—N5 31 R—R3, threatening 32 R—B4 mate* **30 R—R8 K—K2 31 B—N6** Black resigned.

Index of Photographs
and Sketches

Index of Games